Over 200

Talks for All-Age Worship

Susan Sayers

kevin
mayhew

kevin mayhew

First published in Great Britain in 2009 by Kevin Mayhew Ltd
Buxhall, Stowmarket, Suffolk IP14 3BW
Tel: +44 (0) 1449 737978 Fax: +44 (0) 1449 737834
E-mail: info@kevinmayhewltd.com

www.kevinmayhew.com

The Publishers wish to thank all those who have given their permission to reproduce copyright material in this production.

The material in this 2009 edition has previously been published in *100 talks for all-age worship*, *More talks for all-age worship* and *Living Stones* – Complete Resource Book, Year B.

9 8 7 6 5 4 3 2 1 0

ISBN 978 1 84867 166 9
Catalogue No. 1501177

Cover design by Rob Mortonson
Edited by Peter Dainty
Typeset by Rob Mortonson

Printed and bound in Great Britain

Contents

Foreword

It is common practice in modern churches for the whole church family, from the youngest to the oldest, to come together for at least part of morning worship. This may be for a few minutes at the beginning or ending of the service, but there will also be times when the whole of worship is shared by all ages. One of the most challenging and potentially exciting aspects of such worship is the opportunity it provides for the proclamation of the Gospel and the presentation of Christian teaching in stimulating and refreshing ways.

Anyone who has had the privilege of leading all-age worship will be aware not only of its difficulties, but also of its delights – one of which is the strong sense of *sharing* which is sometimes missing from more formal worship patterns. For one thing, there is a shared understanding of the teaching. The Gospel is for all, and can be understood by all when it is expressed in terms of everyday experiences to which everyone can relate at their own level. Jesus himself knew this, and that is one of the reasons why he taught in parables. The ideas in this book aim to present the Gospel message in a way that will mean something to every member of the congregation. The shared understanding which results will have an untold spiritual impact on the corporate life of the church.

Another delight of all-age worship springs from shared participation in the teaching. Movement, speech and action are encouraged; in fact they are essential if the congregation is to feel involved, not only superficially but at a deeper level. Humour will play an important part, but more important will be the greater sense of togetherness and mutual awareness which a more open and uninhibited expression of faith and feeling make possible.

The ideas presented here are only suggestions, of course, and it is to be hoped that they will be adapted to suit the needs of particular churches, or that they will inspire other ideas which will present the Christian message in ways that are both memorable and meaningful. Expect the unexpected – the Holy Spirit can speak to us not only through the carefully prepared words of the minister or leader, but also through the uninhibited comments and actions of children and adults alike, who are learning together what God has to say to his people.

Susan Sayers

About the author

Susan Sayers is one of the most widely published writers on spirituality and worship. Her bestselling all-age resource for Common Worship, *Living Stones,* is used in the majority of parishes.

Susan is an Anglican priest in Essex.

The Lord our God

Describing God

Begin by asking a couple of volunteers to take part in a guessing game. Give one person a note with the name of an animal written on it. This person tries to describe the animal to the other person, who has to guess what the animal is.

If you have access to a flip chart you could get the second person to draw what they hear being described. You could have two or three goes at this, or you could ask everyone in the congregation to pair up and play the game. The way you do it will depend on the expectations and nature of the congregation!

Now fix a cardboard pair of rabbit ears on a volunteer and explain how we all tend to describe things in terms of what we know already. We would probably describe a rabbit as being furry with long ears because our own ears are short, and we are generally lacking in fur. Ask for suggestions as to how a rabbit might describe a human? (It might be something like a bald rabbit with very short ears.)

It's even harder trying to describe someone we have never seen, like God. It's difficult, but we do our best by looking at the world he has created and picking up clues from this. What can we tell about God by (a) looking at his creation? (Write these qualities up for everyone to see.) (b) Looking at Jesus? (Write these qualities too.) (c) Looking at the working of the Holy Spirit? (Add these qualities.)

Because we worship God as Father, Son and Holy Spirit we can find all these qualities in him.

Getting to know God

Begin by talking about how first impressions are sometimes spot on, and sometimes disastrously wrong. We gradually get to know who someone really is by the clues their words and behaviour give us.

Ask a volunteer (of 12 years or over) to come and help. Secretly show them the picture of what they are and then hang the picture on their back so that no one can see it. Invite everyone to ask the volunteer questions to which s/he can only answer 'yes' or 'no'. Keep track of what is found out until eventually the identity is guessed correctly and the volunteer turns round to reveal that s/he is indeed who they thought.

What on earth has this to do with our theme?

The fact is that we get to know Jesus in exactly the same way – bit by bit we start to discover his character by seeing how he acts towards people in the Gospel. Bit by bit we learn that he is revealing God's nature to us, until eventually we can say for certain that he truly is the Son of God.

It's the same with our experience of the living God. Gradually as we keep in close touch with him we get to know him better and recognise wonders in our lives which are typically God's doing. Perhaps we've been praying and praying for God to sort out a problem, and then events start coming together in a way which is totally different from what we had in mind, but solves the problem in a better way than we could have hoped for. And we thank God very fondly and affectionately, because we recognise that it has been a typical God-response to our need, and we have got to know him better in the process.

But we must seek him; we would never have found out who the volunteer was unless we had asked and used our curiosity and imagination. If we walk through this week more alert, attentive and expectant, we shall notice the signs of glory we may have been missing.

Mr God

Bring with you a few Mr Men books – *Mr Muddle, Mr Bump* and *Mr Chatterbox,* for instance – and invite the children to help you explain to the adults why they are called those names. Point out how they look just like their names and their characters. In those stories we put shapes to ways of behaving. Meeting the characters helps us understand what it's really like to be muddled, accident-prone or extra chatty.

The Bible looks at the same kind of idea. To help us understand more about what God is like, we meet aspects of his nature as characters. We are introduced to Miss Wisdom (Proverbs 8:11-31) and Mr Word (John 1:1-14).

Miss Wisdom shows us how wise God is. It isn't just a question of knowing lots of clever things (though God is all-knowing). Miss Wisdom is described as being beautiful, happy, and excited by all the loveliness of creation, enjoying it almost like a good friendship. So we now know that God's nature is like that.

Then, in John 1:1-14, we meet Mr Word. We are told he's been around as long as God has. From his name we would expect Mr Word to be telling us something, as that's what words do. And we'd be right, because that's exactly what Mr Word does. Mr Word is a person whose life tells us exactly what God is like. (Show a large version of the picture below.)

He's a bit like a human speech bubble – which God himself is speaking. And although we may not usually call him by his name of Word, we do actually know him already quite well. He is Jesus, God's Mr Word, who was born as a baby at Christmas, and lived on earth loving, healing and teaching, very wisely.

The mind of God

Beforehand make three large card signs on which are written: GOD MIND S.

First ask three volunteers to hold the signs up in this order: GODS MIND and explain that this morning we are going to think about the way God's mind works: how God thinks.

Ask if anyone knows what you are thinking. They might be able to guess, but really our thoughts are very secret, unless we choose to give people clues to how we're thinking. Mime being angry about the choice of one of today's hymns, and see if anyone can then work out from this what is in your mind. Then mime something which shows you are pleased or surprised. (These could all be linked with the hymn numbers if you wish.)

Explain that God does want us to understand what's in his mind, so he gives us clues which we see in the things he has made. We know from the way the universe works, for instance, that God must be very careful and imaginative, enjoy lots of variety, like order and harmony, and consider everything important, from the largest to the tiniest item.

Ask the volunteers to rearrange themselves so that the message now reads: GOD MINDS. God cares about us and all his creation; he bothers about how we are feeling and what we are doing. He hurts when we hurt and aches when we mess our lives up for ourselves and those close to us. He is overjoyed when we find real happiness and delight with him in the way things are designed to be. If we want people to be really clear about what is in our mind, we talk, and explain how we are feeling and what we are thinking. And God does that, too. Jesus is often called the Word of God, and through Jesus' words we can find out clearly what is in God's mind. All through the gospel we get the message that God minds. He knows everything we think and say and do, and minds about it.

Taste and see

Begin by having the following read out, or having it printed on the weekly sheet. It is an extract from *The Solitaire Mystery* by Jostein Gaarder.

'Tell me about Rainbow Fizz,' I said. He raised his white eyebrows and whispered, 'It has to be tasted, my boy.'

'Can't you tell me what it tastes like?'

He shook his old head in despair.

'A normal fizzy drink tastes of orange or pear or raspberry – and that's that. That isn't the case with Rainbow Fizz, Albert. You taste all those flavours at the same time with this drink, and you even taste fruits and berries you've never been near with your tongue.'

'Then it must be good,' I said.

'Hah! It's more than just good. You can taste a normal fizzy drink only in your mouth . . . first on your tongue and the roof of your mouth, then a little bit down your throat. You can taste Rainbow Fizz in your nose and head, down through your legs, and out through your arms.'

'I think you're pulling my leg,' I said.

'You think so?'

The old man looked almost dumbfounded, so I decided to ask something which was easier to answer.

'What colour is it?' I asked.

Baker Hans started to laugh. 'You're full of questions, aren't you, boy. And that's good, but it's not always easy to answer. I have to *show* you the drink, you see.'

Talk about how hard it is to describe something so wonderful that it is impossible to imagine; the only way Albert is really going to find out how wonderful Rainbow Fizz is, is to experience it for himself.

It's a bit like that with God. We can't really imagine how wonderful he is till we've experienced him for ourselves. If you ask anyone who has become aware of the great, loving God working in their life, they'll agree that there really aren't any words to describe how wonderful and amazing he is. They just know because they've experienced him in action.

In Mark 1:29-34 we hear how Jesus went to the house of Peter and Andrew, where he was staying. Peter's mother-in-law had a bad fever and was very ill, and Jesus made her better. After she'd made them all supper, full of new energy, no doubt, crowds of visitors came, all wanting

Jesus to heal them as well. So he did. Through Jesus, God was working right there in those people's lives, and making them more free and happy than they had ever felt before. It was so exciting to see! We can imagine how happy it made Jesus to see these people suddenly realising at last how wonderful God was! He couldn't wait for everyone else to find out.

Well, people are still finding out that our amazing God can set us free to live happy and joyful lives doing good and standing up for what is right and true. And how are they going to discover God? Only if those of us who have found out already how wonderful he is are prepared to tell them about him, and introduce them to him.

God rules – OK?

Unless the size of your congregation makes it far too expensive, give everyone a penny. Invite everyone to look at their coin. On one side there is a picture of someone's head. Whose head is it? It belongs to Queen Elizabeth II. She is there, just as Caesar's picture was on the coin Jesus looked at (see Matthew 22:15-22), because she is the Head of State and we are her subjects. In our country there are taxes to pay to make sure that everyone, both rich and poor, can have schools, roads and hospitals. There are laws to keep, so that we can all live safely and peacefully, and there are police to check that we keep the laws. Those who break them are sent to prison or charged a fine.

Each country works out its own way of organising all this, and some are fairer than others. Each country has leaders – people who are in charge – and the country Jesus lived in was ruled by the Romans.

Now invite everyone to hold their coin in the palm of one hand. This penny is not very big. It won't buy very much. It sits here in your hand, and your hand is here in this church building. It's only a very little part of all the space in here. As you hold your penny, your hand is surrounded not just by the space of this building but by the whole universe. Now God is greater than the universe, because he is the One who thought and loved our universe into being.

There's a huge, huge difference between the kind of power and authority human leaders have, and the kind of power and authority God has. We are to give to God what is God's. What is God's? Is there anything God doesn't know? No. Is there anywhere God can't reach? No. Is there anything or anyone God doesn't care about? No. God is much greater and more wonderful than we can imagine, and he holds all creation in the palm of his hand, like you are holding the little penny in the palm of your hand.

No wonder we've all chosen to come and spend some time praising him this morning! God is worth everything we can ever give him.

Of course, we are to respect our leaders, and keep the laws. We are to be good citizens, just as our Christian rule of love tells us. But we also need to remember who is ultimately in charge, and put God first. We need to be prepared to make a fuss if any laws are passed which are against God's law, and we need to do what we can to help our leaders uphold the authority of the God who made us all.

God's point of view

Ask for two volunteers. Stand one on a chair and have the other lie down on the floor. Talk with the volunteers about what they can see from their particular viewpoint. Although nothing else in the church has changed, the descriptions will be different because of where the volunteers are.

You could also suggest that everyone looks at something central, first through one eye and then the other. They can then all notice the change of view even when looking out from the same head!

We need to get into the habit of looking at everything from God's point of view. What we then see may sometimes come as a surprise to us, because we are so used to looking from our own point of view. Take Joseph, for instance (see Matthew 1:18-25). He was in for a surprise. He thought he had worked out the kindest way of dealing with the embarrassing problem of Mary expecting a baby before they were married. He had it all worked out. He'd divorce Mary without a big fuss, so that she needn't be noticed too much.

But through the dream God helped him look at things from another point of view. Joseph saw that Mary's baby was all part of God's plan, and, rather than divorcing her, he had an important job to do – to look after Mary and this very special baby. Joseph must have been a very brave man, as well as a good and kind one. He knew people would think he was stupid; perhaps they would stop being friends with him; his life would never be nice and straightforward again. But he did that brave, good thing because he had seen the situation from God's point of view and was happy to go along with that.

It was the same with Mary (see Luke 1:38). If she had only seen the angel's message from her own point of view she might have refused to go along with God's plan, which was bound to turn her own hopes and dreams upside down. But she saw it from God's point of view – that the people of our earth needed a Saviour; God needed to be born as a human baby so he could rescue humans as an insider. And a baby needed a mum. So she agreed and that made Christmas possible.

The unknown God

Start by displaying a fairly simple equation, such as $2x+3=x+10$, or $y(5+2)=21$, or $x+4=6$ (difficulty depends on your congregation), perhaps on a blackboard. Provide chalk, and ask someone mathematical to take us through the stages of solving the mystery of this unknown value of *x* or *y*.

When Paul was in Athens he saw an altar to 'the unknown god', and set about explaining to the people who this God was (see Acts 17:22-23). It was as if the people had been calling God '*x*'. Now when we tried to solve our *x* mystery, we worked it out, step by step, gradually getting a clearer idea of what *x* meant, until, in the end, it was quite clear to us (or some of us!).

That's rather like the way we can look at the beauty and order of our world, and all the physics and chemistry of it, and all the variety and colour and shape in it, and begin to work our way towards discovering what God is like. We can work out that he must be clever and thoughtful, and imaginative and faithful, for instance.

But with Jesus coming, and showing us exactly what God is like, it's more like this.

Set up the same equation as before, using solid shapes, like building blocks. Each *x* is a bag, filled with the correct number of blocks. We could still work out what *x* is, but if the bag is opened, we can actually see what it is. (Do this.)

With Jesus' life there in front of us through reading the Gospels, and through living in his company every day, we can have a very clear idea of what God is like. We can see that he is forgiving and totally honest and good, that he is responsible and stands up for what is right, whatever happens to him and however much people sneer. We can see that he looks for the good in people and doesn't condemn them or give up on them. We can see that his love has been proved stronger than death.

If we put our faith in that God, whom Jesus has revealed to us in a new and clear way, and if we claim to love him, then we will have to start doing what he says. Who finds it easy to be obedient? Most of us find it very hard. We don't want to do what we are told; we want to do what we like!

Jesus says that the way you can tell if someone really does believe in him and love him, is by whether they are obedient to him, and obey what he says. That means listening to God and saying yes to him, whether it's what we want to do or not.

That is a *very* hard thing to learn, but it's worth learning, because being friends with Jesus is the best and happiest thing that could ever happen to us.

The stamp of God

Bring along a rubber stamp and ink pad, making sure it isn't permanent ink. Begin by putting the stamp on a number of volunteers. Talk about the way we sometimes get stamped at theme parks or discos to show that we have a right to be there because we have paid our entrance fee.

When we are baptised we have the sign of Jesus Christ marked on our foreheads. (What is that sign? It's the cross.) It's as if we've got God's stamp on us. (You could get everyone to trace a cross on their foreheads with their thumb to feel it freshly.) We are marked out as his children, whether we are one-day-old children, twenty-three-year-old children or ninety-seven-year-old children, and we have been freely given the right to belong in God's kingdom, which is a kingdom full of love and peace and joy, patience and kindness, goodness, gentleness and self-control.

As well as us belonging in God's kingdom, God's kingdom now belongs in us! As we've got God's stamp on us we will be wanting to behave like him, and he will help us to do that. Our behaviour will then be a visible sign to other people that we really do belong to God as his children. When they see us being honest and kind and patient and joyful, loving and working for peace and justice, they will be able to say, 'That must be a child of God – look how generous he is, even when he isn't going to gain anything by it!' And, 'That must be a child of God – look how loving she is with those difficult people!'

The whole point is this: we don't work to behave nicely so that God will love us. We don't need to do that, and we can't ever earn his love anyway. God simply loves us! He thinks we're really special, and he always wants the best for us.

When we love him back, and let him work in us, we will find we are beginning to behave more like our God. The closer we get to God, the more generous loving we will find ourselves doing. Instead of looking out for what we can get all the time, we'll find we're looking out eagerly for ways we can give instead! Instead of making sure we are doing whatever *we* want, we'll find we are looking to check if other people are OK. And that is actually a much happier and more fulfilling way to live.

God of fire

Strike a match and light a candle. Talk about how useful fire is to heat up food and cook it, to keep us warm, melt steel and make steam to generate power. But fire is very powerful, and so it can be very dangerous. Show a picture or a model of a fire engine, and enlist the children's help in talking about what happens when fires get out of control, and how the firemen fight the dangers. We need to have a healthy fear of fire to keep us safe.

God is very powerful. When you think of the power needed to create fire and oceans, ranges of mountains and galaxies of stars, you can't help but be a bit fearful at the thought of getting in touch with such a powerful person.

We are sensible to stand in awe of this great Being, on whom we depend for everything, including life itself. We are right to respect the Lord of life, and think carefully before we speak to him, and give him our full attention whenever we pray. We are right to humble ourselves in his presence and behave well during church services. God sees everything we do and knows everything we think, both the things we are pleased about and the things we are secretly rather ashamed of. Sometimes we behave as if God is more of an easygoing pet than the Lord of the entire universe. We need to take God seriously and recognise that he is very powerful indeed.

(Pick up the candle again.) But that great power of God is only part of the story. Just as a candle is a person-sized fire, which we can hold and which gives us light, but doesn't frighten us like a house on fire, so Jesus is the way we can approach the great creative God in person.

God speaks our language

Beforehand ask a couple of computer crazy people to work out a very short conversation using as much jargon as they can fit in. If you have any Latin or Greek scholars, ask them to work out a brief conversation in that language, and if you have a couple of teachers, ask them to do a short discussion using all the technical attainment targets jargon. Of course you may have different skills and interests among your congregation, so home in on any kind of language which means everything to those in the know and nothing whatever to anyone else.

Begin by introducing the two or three conversations as if they are really going to help people. Then admit that you haven't actually understood very much yourself, and no doubt they haven't either. Language can sometimes block our understanding; church language can sometimes make visitors feel like aliens visiting a strange planet, if it is too different from ordinary language that we use every day. Some of the older translations of the Bible, though beautiful to those who have grown up with them, can make a new reader suppose that Jesus has nothing in common with their own time, and only speaks in a language they don't understand.

But of course that isn't true. Jesus spoke to the woman at the well in a way that she understood so clearly that she shot off and dragged all her friends along to meet him (John 4).

When God makes himself known to you it will be in a way that you, personally, understand, because he knows you and loves you. He knows what makes you tick, what you are afraid of, what you hate doing and what you enjoy. He knows what you've been through in your life, what you can cope with easily and what you find very hard. So as he walks with you through each moment of each day right through death and beyond, he will explain things to you, comfort you and give you a nudge in ways which exactly suit your character and situation. All we have to do is live each day expecting him to be in touch, so that we recognise his voice.

He may speak during your prayer time by ideas that suddenly come and will solve a problem in a way you hadn't thought of before. He may speak by something from your Bible reading suddenly hitting you with fresh and very personal meaning. He may speak through events that happen through the day, so that you understand them as picture language which God uses to teach you something he wanted you to learn or understand. He may speak through a conversation you have, or even overhear.

So often, though, God takes us by surprise, and we need to be prepared for that in case we think it can't be God because he's not following our rules. God made this whole universe, so nothing at all is unusable. Keep your ears open, then, and be ready to listen whenever your God speaks.

Messages from God

Begin by giving out a few messages as if they are notices, rather like this. 'Is Ali Holden here? I've got a message from Molly, your neighbour's dog. She says when you next take her for a walk could you go past the swimming pool as there are some good smells around there. And then there's another message . . . this is for John Bendkowski. It's a message from the rope you used to climb the tree, asking for another high level outing as it enjoyed the view.' (Use inside information so that the messages match up with real life.)

What do we reckon – are those messages true or not? Does Ali take a dog called Molly out for walks? Did John use a rope to climb a tree? Yes! Then what makes us think the messages aren't quite right? It's because common sense tells us that dogs and ropes can't send messages like that, even if they wanted to. Today we are looking at the way God calls us, and how we can work out whether it's really God calling us, or not.

What first alerted Ali and John to the messages given out? It was their names. When God calls us, he gets our attention and speaks directly to us. Sometimes what happens is that we hear a reading at church, or read a passage of the Bible at home, and suddenly a particular bit hits home, and we know it's meant specially for us. It's as if it has our name on it. God spoke into Jonah's heart so that Jonah knew God had a message for him, whether he chose to obey it or not. The fishermen heard Jesus calling directly to them as they worked in the fishing boats. So one thing we can learn about God's call is that it feels personal to us.

The next thing to look at is this: is this the sort of message that God would give? With our messages from a dog and a rope, we knew they didn't ring true, so we could laugh at the messages and not take them seriously. But what other things might make us suspect that a call is not from God at all? If it's to do with anything unkind, violent, selfish, greedy, lazy, deceitful, or evil, then the call we think we are hearing is not coming from the God of truth and love. But if we feel God is calling us to something loving, selfless, thoughtful, kind, courageous, honest, or good, then it's likely that God is speaking into our hearts, and we should listen carefully.

Then what? The first time Jonah heard God, he chose to run away from what he was asked to do. That ended up with him being tipped overboard and swallowed by an enormous fish! The second time God called, Jonah chose to do what God wanted him to do, even though he really didn't like the idea very much (see Jonah 3:1-4). When Andrew and Simon Peter, James and John heard Jesus calling them, they got up straightaway, left everything and followed him to do what they were being called to (see Matthew 4:18-22). If we hear God calling us, and we choose not to listen, or not to obey the call, the terrible truth is that people who might have been helped won't be; people who might have been saved might not get the chance God wanted them to have.

So we need to be ready to hear God calling in the quiet of our hearts, check with our experience of God that the call is true, and then be prepared to obey the call, going bravely wherever God is leading us.

Listening to God

Begin by telling everyone you are going to drop a pin. Ask people to raise their hand if they hear it. (If the building is large, choose something slightly noisier to drop.) Point out how they all listened to be able to hear it. Today we are thinking about careful listening. Tell everyone you are going to drop the pin again, and this time ask them to notice what their bodies are doing to hear such a little sound. When you have dropped the pin, collect some of the things people have noticed. (These might include things like concentrating, waiting, being very still, cutting out our own noises, putting our best ear forward, turning our hearing aid up a bit.)

God is often revealed or shown to us through the scriptures – through the words in the Bible. (Hold a Bible and open it as you talk about it.) In Nehemiah 8:1-10 we hear how all the people gathered in the square in front of the temple and had God's law read out clearly to them so they could really understand it. And when they heard it like this, they couldn't wait to start living the way they knew God wanted them to live. The reason they heard God's voice that day was because they were really trying to listen, like us trying to hear the pin drop.

When Jesus went to preach at his local synagogue (see Luke 4:16-22) he taught the people that the prophecy from Isaiah was coming true that very day. The ones who were listening as carefully as you listened for the pin dropping would have been very excited. Jesus was giving them a very strong clue about who he really was. And it isn't every day you have the promised Messiah turning out to be someone you grew up with!

The trouble is that lots of them weren't listening at all. And in our lives we are often so busy and preoccupied with things that don't really matter that we make too much noise to hear the still, small voice of God telling us really important things about what is right and what is wrong, and how we can live good lives, full of honest, loving behaviour.

God will always whisper what is good and true and loving to help us. We won't hear an actual voice because God can speak straight into our hearts and minds, so we will just know, suddenly, that what we are doing is very good or very bad, very thoughtful or rather selfish and unkind. Once we know, we can stop the wrong behaviour and change it. But we do need to get used to listening so we can hear God clearly.

God's warnings

Place around the church such warning signs as, 'Wet paint' on a chair, and 'Wet floor' next to a bucket and mop. Ask a couple of volunteers to go round the church to find the signs and bring them to you. Warnings are very useful! What would we do if we saw the 'Wet paint' sign? Avoid sitting on the chair. That's useful because it means our clothes don't get spoiled. What would we do if we saw the 'Wet floor' sign? We'd make a point of walking carefully, instead of running, so that we didn't slip on the wet floor and hurt ourselves.

It's quite normal for prophets to speak out God's warnings to his people, and Micah is no exception (see Micah 3:5-12). He doesn't mind that his message is going to be unpopular, any more than Jesus minds speaking out the truth. That's because he knows that warnings from God may help people sort out what is wrong in their life, say sorry to God for it, and ask his help to put things right as best they can. He tells his hearers the things they need to sort out and change. If they listen, and really start to repent, or turn their lives around, they will be able to work with God to put things right. Otherwise, they will end up with their holy city being destroyed.

Jesus warned his disciples that Jerusalem was going to be completely destroyed, even before some of them had died, because people had taken no notice of all the warnings they had been given (see Matthew 24:1-14). Jesus was talking in about AD 32, and over the next forty years all those earthquakes, wars and plagues happened in the area. In AD 70 the Romans stormed the city of Jerusalem and destroyed it completely, just as Jesus had foretold.

Warnings are useful, and we need to take notice of them. Some of us have been shown films to warn us about the dangers of smoking and drugs and AIDS, and we are warned each summer to protect our skin from sunburn. The captain on the *Titanic* was warned that too much speed could be dangerous. These warnings are there to help us, but we do need to listen to them and act on them if they are going to work.

It's just the same with our spiritual health and well-being. Show a torch and a ruler. God gives us his light to see by, and his truth to measure our lives by. If we become aware of God warning us about our attitudes or behaviour or our relationships, we need to take it on board and do something about it before it's too late.

Standing with God

Ask if anyone is brave enough to stand up on their own and say, 'I am a Christian'. Have a few people from different ages to do this and recognise that we don't find it easy to stand up on our own and admit our faith, even here among friends. No wonder we find it so hard to stand up and say what we believe when we are among people who disagree, sneer at God, or may think we're weird.

Ask three people to come and stand out in front while everyone else suddenly stands up and points at them. We often feel like them – very small and vulnerable – when we find ourselves the only Christians around, or when we are feeling very strongly tempted to do wrong, and so we keep quiet when we could be speaking out against evil, or we try and avoid going where our faith will be challenged.

But what did the prophet say to the King of Israel (1 Kings 20:28)? (Display these words: 'I will deliver this vast army into your hands, and you will know that I am the Lord'.) Ask all the people to be the prophet and whisper these words to the few in the front. Emphasise that these words are true; we are fighting against evil and the evil is certainly powerful, but we are fighting in the power of God, who is far more powerful and in his strength we can be brave.

God's harvest

Have ready a good supply of inflated balloons on strings. These will be needed later.

Bring out three sweets or apples and explain that three people are going to get them. Give them out completely randomly and then ask if that was fair. Agree with them that it wasn't fair, and often life seems unfair to us. (This is something that all ages know about.) Explain how our world is full of injustice and sometimes cruel and terrible things happen which don't make sense.

Now ask anyone who would like a balloon to raise a hand. Invite these people to come and collect a balloon and return to their seats. You will need them to gather with their balloons later on, when you beckon them.

As Christians we don't have to pretend the bad things aren't there, or try to work out easy answers that don't make sense. God knows there are sad and bad things happening in our world as well. They happened just the same when Jesus was walking around in Galilee. A tower fell on some people and killed them (see Luke 13:4, 5). The people asked Jesus to explain it, but he didn't. He felt very, very sorry for anyone who was ill or whose child had died, but, instead of explaining why, he set about comforting them and doing everything he could to make things better. So that's what we need to do as well while we are alive.

But Jesus did tell us that life wouldn't always be unjust. One day, he said, everything as we know it will finish, and on that day everything you, and everyone else, have ever done which is good or kind, or helpful, friendly or honest will be gathered in, like harvest, and kept (see Matthew 13:36-43). (As you say this, gather all those with balloons together in the centre.) It will be an exciting and very beautiful harvest!

Let's make sure that we grow plenty of love and thoughtfulness and honesty and integrity in our lives, however old or young we are, so that whenever that last day comes, we'll be helping to make it a bumper harvest.

God's wonderful party

Bring with you a sealed envelope containing an invitation to a very special party or wedding. The date for the celebration needs to say 'to be arranged'.

Tell everyone how you have received this letter, and it looked so exciting that you thought you'd bring it to church and open it there. Invite someone to come and help you open the envelope, and someone a bit older to read it out. Show your excitement and start planning what to give as a present, and what to wear, getting suggestions from people and scribbling it all down on a list. Such a lot to think about!

Then stop as you ask to check the date of the celebration. Realise that it only says 'Date to be arranged'. *Date to be arranged!* That means you have no idea when to get ready. It might be ages to wait. It might be next week! Suppose it's next week!

Come to the conclusion that the only way you can be sure to be ready is to get ready straight away.

Put the invitation down and pick up a Bible. As you flick through the pages talk about how you are sure there is an invitation to a party somewhere in here as well. Find Isaiah 25:6-9 and read it out.

It's going to be quite a day, and we'll need to make sure we're ready for it. But what was the date again? Look and find it's another case of 'Date to be arranged'. Only God knows the actual date. That means it could be a long time ahead or it could be very close, so the best thing to do is to get ready straight away.

What kind of presents would be in order for this party?

Collect ideas like loving kindness, peacemaking, compassion, forgiveness, goodness and self-control. If we start now, we can grow those in our lives.

What kind of clothes would be suitable?

Clean clothes and good habits like honesty, faithfulness, humility, just or fair behaviour, and thoughtfulness. If we haven't got any yet, we can go to God's wardrobe and he'll make them to fit us perfectly. And if we have got them, but haven't worn them lately, now is the time to get them out and put them on again. These clothes get more and more beautiful as you wear them.

God's great day will be a wonderful celebration, and whether we are alive here or the other side of death, we will all be able to see it and take part.

God's everlasting kingdom

Bring in something to show which you thought would last you a long time, but hasn't (like a pair of shoes or a felt-tip pen), and something else which you didn't think would last at all and it has (like a paper bookmark or a jar of Marmite). Talk about these and the way some things, like great cathedrals, are built to last for hundreds and hundreds of years, while other things, like newspapers or toilet paper, are not designed to last very long at all.

King David wanted to build a temple for the glory of God which was a strong, permanent structure, rather than a temporary tent. And God told David that his ideas for the kingdom were far more long-lasting even than a strong building; God's idea was for a kingdom of love and peace that would last not just for a long time but for ever and ever and ever. And Jesus would be the king. The angel Gabriel was sent to Mary to tell her all about it.

'You are going to have a child, Mary,' said Gabriel, 'and he's going to be the king of a kingdom that will last for ever.' The angel even told Mary what to call her child when he was born. (Show a large notice with the word 'Jesus' on one side of it.) He was to be called Jesus.

Names are important, and they often have a special meaning. Pick out some of the names in the congregation and look up what they mean in one of those 'your baby's name' books. The name Jesus has a meaning as well. It means 'Saviour: the one who saves' (show this written on the other side of the Jesus sign). Through King Jesus, God was coming to save his people.

When Jesus, the Saviour King, was born at the first Christmas, that was just the beginning! God's kingdom is still here today, and it's still growing.

A to Z

Beforehand prepare a long length of lining paper on which the alphabet is written clearly. Fix it up where everyone can see it, or ask people to hold it. (Please don't make them hold it high or their arms will drop off!)

Claim that on this sheet you have the whole of the Bible, the complete works of Shakespeare, every love letter ever written, every postcard and Christmas letter ever sent. You also have the names of every person and every place.

At this point a pre-arranged person walks out to protest. Preachers are supposed to tell the truth and here you are telling porky pies. You can't possibly have all that on this sheet of paper. You've only got a few letters!

Meet the challenge by inviting them to find their own name from the sheet, which they spell out letter by letter, and have to admit that they are on the sheet after all. Get someone else to find 'To be or not to be' and 'Come, Lord Jesus'. These are also found to be there.

Our God is like A to Z – the beginning and the end of everything, all thoughts and ideas, all creation, all love, all hope, all existence (see Revelation 1:8). That's why we worship God – God has always been. God is, at this very moment now. (Pause for everyone to become aware of that amazing fact.) And God will always be, for ever. God's kingdom is wherever Jesus reigns as our King. And that means wherever people say, 'Yes!' to Jesus, 'I really want to be in your kingdom!'

And we know what being in Jesus' kingdom is like, don't we? It's full of love and joy and peace, full of forgiveness and patience, full of hope and healing. Today it's as if we've brought out our flags to wave as we celebrate Jesus as our wonderful, everlasting King, who sets our lives dancing!

God our helper

Living in God's strength

Have a very large, heavy suitcase or box, and make up a short, preferably funny, reason for it being there. Explain that it's extremely important to get this thing moved to the back of the church (or even up to the balcony, if you have one). Invite a small person to come out. Who thinks this person will be able to do it? Let them try, but intervene before any ruptures threaten! What we need is someone really strong. If there are any weightlifters among the uniformed organisations, now is the time for them to be put to the test.

Everyone watches as strength (or combined strength if necessary) achieves the desired effect.

In our lives we often find we have heavy weights to carry. Weights like being left out of the group at school; missing someone we love because they have moved away or died; weights like financial problems, illness or guilt about something we did years ago. (You could have heavy dustbin bags to represent all these.) We find them difficult because we try to lift them with our own strength and all we do is strain ourselves.

Our God is so powerful – he has all the strength needed to carry any weight, no matter how heavy. So the obvious, sensible thing is to let him. Stop saying to God, 'No thanks, I'm fine . . . I'll manage . . .' Stop saying to God, 'You lived ages ago, and I need help now!' Jesus *is* alive right now, full of power, full of good ideas, full of sympathy and understanding. He loves you, he knows your burden already, and he's happy to carry it so you can be free of it.

God to the rescue

You will need a fairly large globe. You may choose to use a few slides of stars and planets (and a projector) as well.

Begin by talking about those times when you're watching a quiz programme or a football match and the people you are watching are making terrible mistakes. You may shout advice at them on the telly, but they don't seem to take any notice of you!

I suspect that might be a little like God feels, as he watches the people he has made messing up their own and other people's lives, and taking not a blind bit of notice of him, even though he could make their lives so much richer and more peaceful.

Now show some pictures of the extent of God's majesty and/or the globe, getting people's help with naming the other planets in our solar system, the name of our sun and our galaxy. Aim to get across the size, beauty and order of God's creation and therefore of the creator himself.

Use the globe to look at the littleness of our world and the separate countries. God has made us free to choose good and evil, and we were getting ourselves and each other into a mess we couldn't get out of. God was prepared to lay all that greatness and majesty aside so as to rescue us by being born, and walking around as a human, loving us back to freedom again.

God's protection

You will need a couple of baby care items, designed for the child's protection (such as a playpen, stairgate, reins or baby alarm). You will also need large signs saying: EGYPT, BETHLEHEM and NAZARETH.

First show everyone the items you have brought, and ask some parents and babies to demonstrate how they are used, reminding people as they watch those aged two and under that Jesus was about this age when Herod's soldiers came to kill him.

Parents spend a lot of effort making sure that their young are safe – as we get older we sometimes think they're fusspots, but their concern for our safety grows out of their love for us. It is because God, our parent, loves us so much that he promises to look after us for ever. Now ask for three volunteers to be Joseph, Mary and Jesus (young toddler) – preferably a family. Ask three other people to be road signs, standing in different parts of the building. (You could use a balcony for Egypt, if there is one.)

Ask the family to start at Bethlehem. King Herod felt threatened by this small boy, so God kept him safe by having him in a family and warning Joseph of the danger of staying in Bethlehem. Joseph listened and acted straight away, rushing his family off to Egypt. (They rush to Egypt.) While they were there Herod died, but his successor was just as cruel so they didn't go back to Bethlehem, they went to Nazareth, which is where they settled.

God may be trying to use us as part of someone's rescue plan. He won't be able to unless we listen to him and do what he wants, whether we understand the reasons or not (see Matthew 2:13-15, 19-23).

God's practical help

Bring with you a small loaf of bread, a pillow, a calendar and a clock, writing paper and envelopes, and a briefcase. Place these prominently around the church.

Begin by reminding everyone of how our God hears us laughing and being happy, and is happy for us. He also hears us when we are crying and feeling sad, and his heart goes out to us, and he feels sad for us and quickly comes close to comfort us with his presence. Even if everyone else has let you down and rejected you, God never has and never will.

All of us will have some sad times in our lives, and today we are going to look at how God looks after his friends when they are going through a rough time. So even if you are in a really happy phase at the moment, it's a good idea to be prepared! And if today you are feeling a bit like Elijah (see 1 Kings 19:1-8), exhausted or rejected, vulnerable and unable to see any hope, then God offers his help straight away.

Ask someone to go and find something to eat, and something to sleep on. As they go, explain how God is very practical, and starts by providing our practical needs – in this case, sleep and food. As the body of Christ, we church people can do that for one another.

Ask someone else to collect things to do with time. As they go, tell everyone that God gave Elijah time, and he didn't rush him. So we mustn't rush one another to get over a heartache either. People whose loved ones have died, or whose marriages are broken, for instance, need time, and we, in love, must give it to them, just as God does.

Ask someone to find some things for helping us keep in touch. While they are fetching them, talk about the way God was in contact with Elijah, and we are helped in our troubles if God's people make a point of keeping in contact through the dark days, and don't leave us feeling isolated. That's why sympathy and get-well cards, short visits and short phone calls can be so comforting. People need to know that we are all praying for them, too.

Ask someone to find something you might carry to work. As they collect it, talk about the way God knows when we are ready to move forward, and gives us a job to do. The job he gave the healed wild man in Mark 5:1-19 was to tell the people in the area about what God had done for him. Elijah was told to go back and continue his former work of being God's spokesman. The job God gives is one that only we can do, and it may well put to use the experiences we have suffered, so that they are turned into opportunities for good.

Leave all the objects out to remind people.

By God's grace we are able

You will need a bowl, a potato and an efficient potato peeler, or several sets of these things if the congregation is large.

First arrange for people with bowls and potatoes (but no peelers yet) to stand at intervals around the building, so that everyone can see what's going on. The volunteers can be of any age – a mixture of ages is best.

Now tell everyone that these people have been given an important job to do; they have to peel a potato and they can start straight away. When they can't start because they have no peeler, tell them to use a coin or a key, a credit card or anything they happen to have brought with them. If they can't find anything at all to use they'll have to use their fingernails. After giving them a little time to struggle, point out how we often struggle to live as Christians relying on whatever we happen to have handy, and so we make heavy weather of loving our enemies, forgiving one another or accepting criticism. Actually God never asks us to work at anything without supplying us with the grace we need. Ask if a potato peeler would make this job easier and give out the peelers.

Now they can do a far more effective job, with far less struggle. We will all lead far more effective lives, which show God's glory, if we are open to God and take time to receive his grace, rather than rushing in to work in our own strength. Ask them to put the peeled potatoes in a bowl of water near the door, to remind us as we go out of church that we need God's grace if our lives are to shine with his glory.

God's refreshing love

Bring in some plants in pots, some of which are wilting pretty badly for need of a good soaking. Choose the kind of plants which respond quickly to kind treatment. You will also need a watering can. Place some of the plants in awkward, hidden places in the building.

Begin by displaying your good, healthy plants, and contrast them with the sad-looking ones. Explain how we sometimes feel spiritually dry and thirsty, sometimes wilting in the stress of a deep worry, or something sad happening in our lives.

God is like a gardener who loves his plants – he sees us wilting and comes to pour his love and hope into our lives again. (Water the plants.) Some plants are easy to water, but others, like us, get themselves in really awkward places, miles from the water and difficult to get at. But God doesn't leave them to go on wilting, he goes out to find them and takes lots of trouble to get at them because he loves them, and wants them to be full of life. (Go around watering the other plants.)

There is no area of your life or our world which is beyond the refreshing touch of the loving, powerful God. (Stand all the plants where they can be seen through the service, so that by the end they can be seen to have brightened up.)

Peace with God

Ask everyone to place their hand flat on their tummy. This is often the place where we can tell if we are anxious or stressed, because it feels 'uptight'. When we are at peace, and not tensed-up, this place is where we feel calm and relaxed, and contented. (In fact, one way of calming yourself down is to do what you are doing now, and breathe slowly in and out a few times.)

Religion isn't telling God he is Lord of our life and then behaving as if he is not important. And it isn't going through the motions of worshipping him without showing his love and compassion to other people. It is all about being at peace with God. Ask for two people who are really good friends to come to the front, and talk to them about what it feels like to be with each other. How does being together make them feel? Do they feel worried about how the other friend will treat them? Would they trust their friend with a secret?

Best friends are good news. You are contented and happy to be with them, and are not worried all the time that you might say the wrong thing and offend them, or that they may start being nasty to you, so you need to be ready to hit them back if necessary. You know you can trust them with your secrets, and they won't laugh at you or think you are stupid. Even going through bad experiences isn't as bad if you are both in it together, because you know you will help one another along.

Well, that's what being at peace with God is like, and it has the spin-off effect of making us deeply happy and calm inside – a feeling that, whatever happens, all will be well. In Mark 6:1-13 we're told how Jesus wanted everyone to know this sense of calm assurance and peace and joy in their lives. He knew there were lots and lots of people going around worried and lost, with no peace inside them because they were not at peace with God. And he sent his disciples off to tell them that the kingdom of God was coming very soon, and soon they would be able to have that closeness with God which would give them peace.

Between the two 'best friends' put up a very large piece of cardboard with the word 'Sin' on it. Sin shuts us off from God and from one another. It makes us think of God as our enemy instead of our friend.

We know that Jesus went on to die for love of us all, which knocked that block of sin away between us and God. (Knock the cardboard away.) So now we can all know that lovely closeness to God which gives us real peace and hope, not just when everything is going well for us, but also through the times of suffering.

In God's hands

First ask for two volunteers to take part in a memory game. Explain that you will reel off a list of numbers and then see how many people in church can remember the list. The two volunteers are given biro pens and told to write the numbers down on the palm of their hands as you say them. When you ask if anyone can tell you the numbers, probably the only ones able to will be those who have written the numbers on their hand to remind them.

Isaiah 49:13-16 explains that God never forgets us – it is as if he has our name written on the palm of his hand, so that he is always lovingly calling us to mind. What God offers us is the chance to be yoked up with him as we stumble and plod our way through life. Show everyone a cut-out yoke, and explain how it worked, with the stronger, more experienced animal helping to guide the younger one in the right way so that the load is less painful to carry.

God's building programme

You will need a lot of children's building bricks – separate and/or interlocking ones. Also make a stand-up notice in thin card which says on it: Our God rebuilds and restores us.

First tip all the bricks out on to the floor in front of everyone, and remind them of the rubble of stones which was all that was left of Solomon's glorious temple when the exiles returned to Jerusalem. Ask people to turn to someone near them and tell one another how they would feel in that situation. Now ask for two or three very young people who enjoy building. Set them to work creating a magnificent building, arranging them to face the congregation so that everyone can watch the building progressing. Ask them to carry on building while you talk. Explain how God responded to his people's feelings of sadness/depression/despair/hopelessness, etc., by speaking words of encouragement through his prophet, Haggai.

In a way the temple, so beautifully planned and made, and now in ruins, was rather like humanity – also beautifully planned and made, but also ruined through evil.

God decided on an extremely costly restoration plan: he sent his only Son into the world to put things right from the inside. Through Jesus Christ living in us we are once again restored to the lovely relationship we were meant to have with God. Like living stones, we are all being built up into God's temple (1 Peter 2:5) – and the temple is a place for God to live in. God is not far away somewhere, but right here in and amongst us now.

Thank the builders and place the notice beside their building.

Finding God's help

Beforehand collect four shoe boxes, and in one of them place a pair of binoculars. Ask a volunteer who wears glasses to help you with the talk this morning. Ask her to stand where most people can see her, and put a chair at four points round her, not near enough for her to touch. Blindfold the volunteer, or ask her to close her eyes. On each of the chairs place a box, and in the box containing binoculars place her glasses. Turn her to face another chair. Point out that Helen needs her glasses, and life is very difficult without them. She can't see much (even when she's not wearing a blindfold!) and she feels very vulnerable. We may feel like this if we suddenly lose something important to us. Perhaps our best friend moves, or we lose our job, or we have a row at home, and suddenly we don't know exactly who we are or which way to turn.

The secret is to turn in the right direction, because God is the one who has both power and inclination to help. His motive is ardent love for his precious child. If we turn any other way and walk in that direction, we will face emptiness and disappointment. (Help Helen to turn in each wrong direction, open the shoe box and find nothing.) But if we turn in the right direction – turn towards God and walk his way (turn Helen the right way), then we will find fulfilment, often far more than we dared hope for. (Helen opens the box and finds in it not only her glasses but a pair of binoculars as well.)

With God in danger

You will need a climbing rope and a life jacket, or some other equipment which protects you from danger in dangerous hobbies. Also a DANGER sign.

First show the equipment, talking about what mad things climbers and slalom canoeists get up to. Ask for a show of hands as to who reckons each is a dangerous hobby. Those who do such things rely on their equipment to protect them, even when they are in acute danger. (If you have any free-fallers, white-water enthusiasts, etc., you could interview them briefly about their most scary moment.)

God is our life-line. He is our sure protection when we are living dangerously in his service, and whatever happens to us (even death), we know that we shall be safe in his hands.

What if we roped up together and then walked down the high street, or put on life jackets and then proceeded to do the washing up? It would be ridiculous, wouldn't it! But sometimes we behave like that – we come to church and offer our whole life to God, sing his praise and pray for the world, then go home and live as safely as we can, keeping our faith as quiet as possible and not getting involved with any evangelism if we can help it.

Let's think again: God promises his protection and we love him, so let's take our courage in both hands and really make ourselves available for him to use in whatever ugly situations he may need us to be.

Accepting God's help

Begin with the sketch set out below. After the sketch ask people to say what they thought the sketch was about. Ideas may well come from this which you and I haven't thought of. That is excellent; they may be issues which people in your congregation need to hear. Draw the ideas together – unless we accept our need of help, God can't help us. All the time we reckon there's nothing wrong with us we don't go to a doctor; it's only when we recognise our need of spiritual healing that we start valuing Jesus and listening attentively to what he says.

Drama sketch: At the doctor's.

Have a sign up with the doctor's name on it and the doctor wearing a stethoscope.

A patient walks in with wads of cotton wool plastered over his eyes so that he can barely see. He gropes around, bumping into the wall, and finds his way to the chair, with the doctor guiding him, something like this:

Doc Ah, good morning, Mr Henning! Do take a seat . . . no, that's the table . . . the seat's over to the right a bit.

Patient Alright, alright, I know where I'm going. What do you think I am . . . blind or something?

Doc Now how can I help you?

Patient Help me? How on earth would you be able to help me? Anyone would think there was something wrong with me!

Doc Er . . . Perhaps I could examine your eyes?

Patient *(jumping up)* Oh no you don't! I've heard about people like you. As if I'd trust my eyes to your interfering fingers. They're my own eyes, aren't they?

Doc Well yes, of course, but . . .

Patient There you are then, my eyes are my own private business, thanks very much. Now why don't you get a move on and stamp these library books. *(He puts some books on the table.)*

Doc But Mr Henning . . .

Patient *(getting up and groping round walls to the door)* I don't know . . . the library system isn't what it used to be . . .

Doc *(shrugs his shoulders and shakes his head. Outside there is the sound of a horn blaring, a screech of brakes and a loud cry.)* There's no helping some people!

God can get us into shape

Beforehand prepare a card stencil shape of a circle. Draw the circle outline properly, but when you cut out the circle, make sure it has some very obvious misshapen parts, so that it looks something like this:

Have a flip chart or several large sheets of paper and a thick felt-tip pen ready. Start by explaining that as part of a visual aid today you need to draw a circle, so you've made a stencil to make that easier. Proceed to draw round the stencil and then express your disappointment that the circle isn't any good. Never mind, you can start again and do it properly on a fresh sheet of paper. Unfortunately, this shape goes wrong as well. Ask someone to try using the stencil and see if they can make it work.

When they can't, get people to explain why the circle keeps going wrong. (The stencil is the wrong shape; every time it's used, the misshapes will go on happening.) We sometimes feel rather like this – however hard we try, we find we go on making the same mistakes, messing things up in our lives again and again. We can't seem to help it. However hard I try, I shall always mess up this circle if I go on using this stencil. We need to make a new stencil for it to work properly, and in our lives we need to be made new so that we can't help but live loving, beautiful lives.

Ask a good cutter-outer to put things right, then try again. (Hopefully, this will be successful!) Admire the results of using a stencil which has been made new. In the same way, our lives will start to show good results when we allow God to sort us out. He works on us gradually, every day throughout our lifetime, and as he works on us and renews us, we start emerging as the person God intended us to be.

God sets us free

Beforehand organise some prison bars. This might be a large oven shelf or anything similar.

First ask for a volunteer, who holds the bars in front of their face so that they look imprisoned. Sometimes we feel imprisoned by our family background. It may be that there is a history of cancer in our family, or suicide; perhaps there has been an alcoholic, or someone with mental illness; perhaps, however old we are now, we still remember a childhood experience of being intensely disliked, ignored or abused in some way. These things can imprison us and make us feel frightened and sad – as if we are partly to blame for their poor health, their sin or their weakness, and however sensibly we try to shake that off, it keeps hold of us.

The wonderful news of our God is that he holds no one of us guilty for what happened to our ancestors; Jesus can set you free from all that sadness and fear (take the bars away), so that you can live again and enjoy the life God has given you.

Now once you are out, you are free.

So if God sets us free, does that mean we can go on hurting other people? No, because as God behaves to us – respecting and loving us – we need to behave to others, so as to respect their freedom as well. We can't delight in God forgiving us and then rush out and criticise someone else!

We might hear this and think we know all about this teaching already. But think again – what about when we discuss the service afterwards; do we only mention the boring bits, laugh over the organist's mistakes and huddle with our own friends? And when those around us are using God's name as a swear word, what do we do? (A hint – if you have got into the habit of swearing like this yourself, start turning it into a prayer as you say it.)

God sets us free; let's enjoy that to the full – remember to pass it on.

Trusting God

Show everyone three things: a colander, a calculator and a calendar. Ask a volunteer to tell you which of the three things they choose to find the answer to 637 x 314. Ask them why they made that choice. Try to persuade them that the others might work. Try the sum on the thing they chose (which I am assuming was the calculator – if it wasn't, try someone else!) Are we surprised? No. Why not? Because we know that calculators do sums – we can trust them.

Do we trust God like that or not quite, yet? Think of who or what you go to first when there's a problem; *that* is what or who you trust most.

Salvation is God's gift

Beforehand, fix an apple on to a string.

Begin by setting an impossible task – who can eat the apple without using their hands while the string is being swung about? Several people can try, but make sure no one succeeds!

Then have someone butting into the game and saying something like: 'You're never going to manage that, are you? That's impossible. I can give you an apple myself, if you really want one enough to make a fool of yourself in front of all this lot!'

If the person accepts the offer, they are given an apple from the intervener's pocket. If not, try with the next contender.

That is like we often are with God. We waste our time and energy trying to earn God's love and save ourselves, when actually it's an impossible task, and he's happy to give it to us free. All we have to do is *trust* God and *accept* his offer.

God loves us to the end

Bring along a well-loved and very well-worn companion – teddy or pyjama case. Introduce him to everyone and point out how we can all see just how well loved he is! He bears the signs of being well loved. Probably most of us older ones feel a bit like this – loving has worn us to the shape we are, a bit threadbare and squashed maybe, but perhaps a little wiser and softer and less selfish as a result. Although we know from experience that loving hasn't always been easy, we can say with certainty that it's well worth living lovingly.

Luke 21:25-28 helps us to look ahead to the end of time, when the sky is wrapped up and the moon folded away. It can sound very frightening, to think of everything we know coming to an end. Whenever there are terrible disasters and famines and wars it can feel as if things are spinning out of control – even out of God's control. Is the end going to be some huge ghastly mistake, brought about by our greed and selfishness?

The Bible reassures us that, however it may look as evil grows and temporarily gains the upper hand, God is always ultimately in charge. As we know, God's way is not to crash into our blundering and force us to change so that disasters are prevented. He has given us that great gift of free will, so that we can choose good or evil in the small and large decisions of life. He longs for us to choose the good that will bring us blessing and peace, but is always there weeping with us in the chaos and suffering that evil leads to, ready to redeem it for good.

And it is that buffeted and battered loving which will last and last for ever. The prophet Daniel gives us a lovely picture of that (see Daniel 12:1-3). All those who have guided others in the right path, he says, will shine like the stars of heaven for ever. All the wise leaders will show up brightly for all to see. If we have set ourselves to live lives of faith and love, there is no way we need be frightened by the last days. After the feeding of the five thousand Jesus told his disciples to gather up the fragments so that nothing is lost. That's how it will be at the end; every scrap of goodness and love will be gathered safely in, so that nothing of it is lost.

False gods

Idolatry

Ask for four volunteers to carry four objects in procession from the back of the building, so that everyone can see them as they go past. There is a charm bracelet, or some other superstitious thing; a mirror; a diary; and a wallet. Have the objects displayed at the front.

Explain how God has warned us to be on our guard in case we are tempted to worship other things instead of the one true God. Sometimes we don't realise when we are doing this, so today we are going to check our lives to make sure we really are worshipping God, and not some idol. We may not kneel down in front of trees or golden calves, but these objects give us a clue as to some other ways we may be just as full of idolatry.

Look at each object in turn. The charm bracelet: believing in luck ruling our lives, with the sense that there is no real order or point in it. God is there, but not actually able to do much.

The mirror: our image becomes extremely important to us. It is more vital to do/wear/have the same as everyone else than to be what God wants and plans us to be.

The diary: feeling that we are only valuable if our diary is full and we have to organise every second of our day. We have effectively blocked God from using our time, except for a little space which we control.

The wallet: we love our possessions and comforts, and forget that as Christians we are no longer owners of anything, but stewards.

As the objects are slowly paraded again, ask people to think carefully as to whether any of them have become idols, and ask God to sort their lives out again.

Designer Gods

As people come into church, give them all a pipe cleaner and a piece of string. Begin the talk by asking everyone to design an animal of some kind using the pipe cleaner and string provided. Everyone can hold up their masterpieces for general admiration.

Point out that everyone's creation is different because we all had our own ideas. We might have picked up on certain qualities of real animals, but even the best of our creations is not much like any real animal we might know.

People invent gods to worship rather as we made our animals. Sometimes there are aspects in these gods which are like the real God, but they are not really anything like the one true God who loved us all into being and is the beginning and end of all things.

We cannot pick and choose with God, making him as we feel on any particular day; we cannot make him at all, because he is there already and always has been. What we can do is enjoy him as he is, enjoy him loving us, and enjoy getting to know him better and better.

False images

We all have different images of the people we know and each person is actually all these and more. As we get to know a person better, we keep adjusting our image of them.

As we get to know God better we shall find the same thing – we will gradually be putting right any false images we have of him and be more able to love and worship him as he really is. Sometimes our false images of God have been handed down to us by how we were first introduced to him. There are empty seats here now because some people in our area have rejected what is in fact a false image of God and one of our main tasks is to show people the true God.

Let's look at some of these commonly held false images:

This god is always ready to condemn us and is very severe, very demanding and disapproves of us enjoying ourselves.

This god made the world a long time ago and then lost interest. He's actually rather lazy and lets us get on with destroying ourselves.

This god is rather pathetic; he smiles naively and doesn't understand the real world that we have to cope with. If you ask him for help he'd probably say he'd like to but it's all rather difficult with things as they are.

This god picks on people and makes life terrible for them.

This god is a little slave-magician, who runs round doing everything we ask but is somewhat deaf and forgetful.

Let's be quite clear about this: all these gods are false images and are nothing at all like the true and living God. We need to destroy them. (Either cross them all out or, if you are using paper, tear them up and throw them away.) Thank goodness people who have these images often do reject them. How tragic that they think God is like that – no wonder people decide not to worship him.

So what is our God really like? Write 'The true God is . . .' in the centre and have people adding to the qualities they have discovered him to be.

God is not a robot

If possible, beg or borrow a radio-controlled car for today. If you don't know anyone who owns such a thing devise one using a willing child, and a carton which she holds round her middle like this:

Tell the controlled car (in either version) which way you want it to go and see how it does exactly what you tell it. Parents wish they could do it to their children! Children wish they could do it to their teachers! And sometimes that's the way we treat God – we might say, 'Well, I don't believe in God any more because I asked him to get me a bike and he didn't. That doesn't prove that God isn't there – it proves that God isn't a radio-controlled car or a slot machine or a magic lamp! And that's true. He isn't.

God certainly comes among us as one who serves, but we mustn't presume to take him out of a box in emergencies. God is not our slave, and his way of doing things is much better than ours anyway, because he understands the whole situation and all the people involved. He's rather like a conductor or composer, bringing all the different parts of the orchestra together to make a beautiful harmony.

So what have we learnt today?

- that we can't control God
- that God is in control
- but that God never makes us do what he wants; we are free to choose.

Worshipping the real God

You will need a loaded camera with a built-in light meter and flash. Begin by introducing everyone to your camera and taking two or three photos, focusing on different people and parts of the building each time. Explain that you don't need lots of complicated flash equipment with this camera because it has been designed with the light meter and flash facility built in. That means that whenever you go to take a picture, the camera automatically checks the light and provides extra light if necessary.

God has designed us with a built-in worship facility. Of course the idea is that we use this to worship our maker and, when we do that, the rest of our life settles into a fully satisfying 'rightness' which is good and liberating. But the facility is still there, whether we use it like this or not and we all worship something because that is part of our design. The real question is 'what'?

Look again at the camera as it focuses on a particular person or thing to photograph. I may insist that I'm trying to get a picture of the organist, but if I'm actually focusing on Brown Owl, then that's the actual picture I'm taking and that's the picture I'll get. (Take the picture.) We may say we worship God, but if our hearts and minds are focused mostly on what we look like and wear, or on food, or the luxury bathroom we'd like, or our hobby, or our girl/boyfriends, or work, then the truth is that we are actually worshipping these things, and not God at all.

Today God is reminding us that all these other idols are very poor substitutes for the real thing; let's get our priorities right if the focus has slipped, and really enjoy using our worship facility in the way it was designed to be used – worshipping the God of enormous power who can work wonders in our characters; the God who has always loved us and cherished us right from our conception onwards; the God who loves and honours us even when our hair goes grey and we aren't as fit as we used to be. This God can provide everything we ever need; let's focus our worship on him alone.

God's way

God's way or ours?

Start by showing everyone how you have spoilt something by using it to do what it wasn't designed for – such as a knife for a screwdriver, or scissors as wire cutters. As we are made like God, and God is loving, we only feel that deep-down sense of peace and rightness when we are using our bodies, minds and spirits in the way they were designed to be used.

Now arrange two teams of three people (mixed in age and character) rather like a quiz show. Have each team holding their team name: THE GOD SQUAD and THE SELF SET. Ask a volunteer to be a Christian in the street, on his journey through life. He walks from the back to the front, and every so often you tell him to stop to sort out a problem. Have the first problem read out clearly, then ask each team what their advice would be. The Christian then decides which to accept, and the congregation can express their approval or not by clapping or groaning. Then he continues on his journey until the next problem and so on. It will be best if you think up situations pertinent to your congregation, but here are some suggestions to get you going:

1. The TV news shows a famine and you have just received your pay packet.
2. Your brother/sister has scratched your favourite CD.
3. The grass needs cutting but your friends are round.
4. You're gasping for a drink, and find a purse lying on the pavement.

In conclusion, make the point that if we say we're Christians it must affect the way we behave, but that even if we choose wrongly sometimes, God can still bring some good from the resulting situation.

Juggling

You need to get hold of someone who can juggle (however badly) with two balls today. If the juggler is really bad, rolled up socks will be better than balls as there is less retrieval time!

Explain that the readings have been all about choices, and the way we choose to live our life. We can choose to live life exactly as we want, buying loads of unnecessary clothes, sweets and luxury goods, yet unable to find more than small change for the Christian Aid collection. Or we can choose to live life exactly as God wants, sharing what we have with other people, being happy to help at home, whether we get paid for it or not, and putting all our time and money at God's disposal.

Perhaps we have already definitely chosen one or other of those ways; for many of us, we try to do it this way. (The juggler does his stuff. It's actually better if he keeps dropping the socks.) We try to juggle our choices, so that sometimes we are holding God at the centre of our lives, and sometimes self. As you can see, it doesn't really work. Sometimes we get into a muddle, all tangled up as we try to serve both God and self at the same time. And we never get to hold on to God long enough to get to know him and understand his will for us in our lives. Having self at the centre of your life will make you possessive and bitter, discontented and miserable. Having God at the centre will make you fulfilled, light-hearted and at peace with yourself. Juggling will make you confused. It's time to make the choice.

Choosing God's way

Have ready a musical instrument, such as a violin or trumpet – it needs to be quite a bulky one; a set of football gear, including a football; a large basket of fruit; six envelopes, three of which are labelled GOD'S WAY and the others MY OWN WAY. I will explain what messages are in which envelopes as we go along.

Introduce three volunteers who will be helping with this week's teaching, and explain that God always equips us for any job he wants us to do, but somehow, we often get it wrong.

Perhaps God gives us a musical gift (give the first person the musical instrument). Then we have a choice – are we going to do things God's way or our own way? The person can choose either envelope to open, and whichever one isn't chosen is opened afterwards so that both possibilities are seen.

GOD'S WAY: Use your musical gift to cheer people up and lead them in worship.

MY OWN WAY: Not bother to practise and never play for anyone.

One way gives a blessing to many, the other wastes the gift.

Now provide the second person with all the football equipment, saying as you do so that God may train us for quite a specialised job – perhaps for helping disabled people through living with a disabled person in our family. When the person is all set up, choose which way to go.

GOD'S WAY: Play football for the school.

MY OWN WAY: Go swimming.

We sometimes decide to go our own way, completely ignore the gifts God has given us, and rush off instead to do something for which we are not equipped at all. Then we wonder why it all fails.

Give the last person a large basket of fruit, showing everyone how delicious all the fruit looks. Which envelope will be chosen?

GOD'S WAY: Give some fruit to people in the church who would really like some.

MY OWN WAY: Eat so much that you get tummy ache and let the rest go mouldy.

Sometimes God gives us gifts which feel very nice, and instead of using them as he intends – to share with others – we get greedy and hang on to them.

Finally, let the last person do things God's way, and share out the fruit among the congregation.

A wise choice

Have a show of hands for a few choices – Who's for football, who's for rugby? Who's a lark and loves the early mornings, who's an owl and loves to stay up late? Who's a 'dog' person, who's a 'cat' person?

All these are a matter of choice, and happily we are all different so we all like to choose different toppings on our pizzas, different music to listen to and different colours to wear. It's wonderful and important that we are all different.

But there are some things we can't choose, because it's been decided that there is a collective good way of going on. So we all drive on the same side of the road whatever part of the country we're in; we all go to school and learn how to read and write and do maths and science; we all pay taxes on what we earn so everyone, both poor and rich, can use schools and hospitals and so on.

In Joshua 24:14-27, Joshua wants the people to decide, before they go in to the promised land, whether they really do want to serve the Lord their God or not. He makes it quite clear that they will only be choosing wisely if they do choose to worship God, as he is real and powerful, and the other gods are not. It's a little bit like asking a football team if they are going to choose to play with a football or a matchbox in an international match. There really isn't much point in playing with anything other than the real thing!

In John 6:60-69 we hear of some of the crowds choosing not to walk with Jesus any more because he seemed to be making out that he was the Holy One of God. Jesus asked his disciples if they were going to turn away as well, and Peter spoke for them all, and for us as well. 'Lord, who else could we go to,' he asked, 'seeing that you are the one with the words of eternal life?' When we know that God is real, and that Jesus really is the Holy One of God, what else can we do but make the sensible, wise choice and commit ourselves to following him? That's the wisest, most important choice we make in the whole of our life.

Chosen to do the impossible

Beforehand place a pair of scissors under one seat, a sheet of A4 paper under another, and a piece of paper with 'It's YOU!' stuck with Blu-tack under a third seat. Make sure that these places are filled.

First choose someone, by telling everyone that the chosen person will find a message with 'It's YOU!' written on it stuck to the underneath of their chair. Now you know a little of how Abraham might have felt when he realised God had chosen him. When we find God choosing us, we tend to spend far too much time thinking 'Why me?' and 'I expect he really meant someone else!' Abraham was happy to let God do the choosing. He just got on with being chosen.

Now someone has been chosen, you have a task for them to do. The task is to make an A4 sheet of paper fit round four people. Can it be done? Collect people's suggestions as to what is certainly needed before it's even remotely possible. (Four people and a sheet of A4 paper.) Sometimes God's plans seem just as impossible at first, and we're tempted to give up. But if we trust him, possibilities gradually unfold . . .

Does anyone happen to have a sheet of A4 paper under their chair? What about four people – are there any willing to volunteer? Now we need some scissors – anyone able to help? Point out how an impossible task is gradually becoming possible. Last we need instructions. Hold out an envelope and point out that it has to be received and opened up before it's any use, which is like praying and listening to God. Now the instructions can be followed so that the sheet of paper actually does fit around four people.

And here are the instructions:

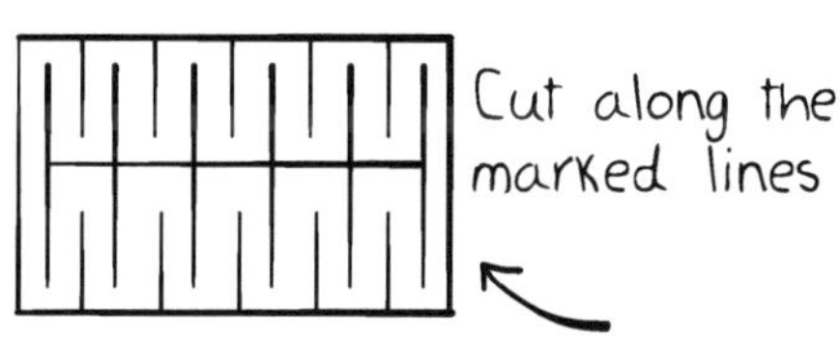

We may be asked to do what seems impossible. But if we trust God he will lead us to the time and conditions where the impossible can happen.

God's hidden agenda

Begin by asking people to forget they know the end of the story of Joshua and the battle of Jericho, and imagine what an unusual set of instructions they must have seemed for taking the city. A bit like being told to walk round your car shouting loudly if you've forgotten your car keys. Perhaps the soldiers thought Joshua was going mad. And yet God knew what he was doing; he knew that the walls weren't as secure as they might have been, and through prayer he allowed Joshua to use this hidden information.

We are used to interpreting things. Show some travel brochures and ask two people to come to the front. One reads an expression you might find inside, and the other reads out what we know it really means:

cosy	=	cramped
quaint and traditional	=	the plumbing doesn't work
very new hotel	=	building loudly in progress
sea view from some rooms	=	sea view from the bathroom

Sometimes we think we have the same agenda as others, but in fact we haven't. Ask two adults and two children to read this out.

Adults	We go for the children's sake.
Children	We go because we're told to.
Adults	It's a nice rest for us all.
Children	They sleep on the beach all day.
Adults	They loved all the animals at the farm.
Children	We loved the slot machine – if you wiggle it you get an extra chocolate bar.

The more we spend time with one another and listen to one another, the less misunderstanding there will be. And it's the same with God. Our ideas are often different from his.

Our idea might be: If I catch this bus I'll be home extra early. But God's idea might be: If she misses this bus she'll meet Mrs Merry and be able to help her with her shopping bags.

Our idea might be: If I don't pass my driving test this time I can always try again – I'm not going to kill myself over it. But God's idea might be: If he does pass this time he'll drive Terry and Pete to Scotland and meet his future wife.

Our idea might be: If I commit myself to a Bible study group I'll miss my favourite TV programme, and anyway, I'm too shy. But God's idea might be: If she goes to a Bible study group I'll be able to help her sort out her shyness, and give her a lifelong friend who will look after her when her mother dies.

Our idea might be: If I make that phone call and he doesn't even remember me I shall look a complete idiot. But God's idea might be: He needs reassurance and encouragement, and she is the most appropriate person to give it – this phone call will stop him falling apart. So if as you pray, God's ideas come to you, be prepared to act on them.

God's music

Beforehand either ask the music group to prepare a short four-part harmony hymn, chant or anthem, or ask three or four instrumentalists to prepare a short piece of music.

First remind everyone that although they are here partly because they chose to come, they are also here because God chose for them to be here, and people praying for them opened the way for God's will to be fufilled.

Ask everyone to sit back and enjoy the prepared music. That is the composer's original plan accomplished, but a lot of people were involved in enabling the composer's ideas to turn into the music which helps us worship. There was the composer, perhaps the composer's teachers, the publisher and the editor, the person at the warehouse who sent his score to the shops, the sales person, and our music director, even before we reach the actual performers. (Have different people to stand out as you mention each job.)

All this is like the way God prepared the ground for the coming of Jesus, right through from Abraham, and including Samuel, who grew up to anoint David as king.

But God also harmonises; he brings things together in the best possible way for everyone. We can get some idea of this if we hear just one strand of the music on its own (just the tenor part, for instance). It's interesting but not riveting! Try another part on its own. There may be times of silence in the separate parts when nothing seems to be happening, just as our prayers sometimes don't seem to be answered, but in fact if there weren't those silences, the whole piece of music wouldn't blend as well as it does.

Ask everyone to listen to the music again, noticing the harmony and remembering how we really can trust God to fulfil his plans in the best way for us.

The covenant

Prepare beforehand a large card with the word COVENANT written on it. Cut the card into two sections along the middle.

Talk about when we go to see plays or films and find we're sitting right behind someone tall, or the row we're in is so far back that we can't see very much at all. We bend our necks to see through the gaps and, just as we catch a glimpse of all the action, someone in front bends over to talk to their friend so that all we see is the back of their heads!

In Exodus 24 we hear about Moses and the people of Israel catching just a glimpse of God's glory on the mountain at the time of God giving the Law and making a covenant with his people. Give out the two pieces of card to two people and ask them to stand one on either side of you, so that everyone can see the cards. Explain what a covenant is by showing how both parties promise something to the other and so both parts need to be kept. When both sides promise (the card pieces are brought together) it makes a covenant; if one party breaks their side of the promise (one person takes their section away) then they are breaking the covenant.

God promised to protect and look after his chosen people, and the people promised to keep God's Law.

Although God always keeps his promise because he is always faithful, people aren't as good at keeping their promise. Sometimes we get so many things in our lives between us and God that they block us off from seeing him clearly. We need to clear away some of those things in our lives so that we get more than a glimpse of God's glory – we need to seek him out so that we get to know him really well and can enjoy his company, as Moses did.

Unwrapping God's law

Begin by reminding everyone of the ten commandments. Have them written up and uncover them one by one as people say them. Point out how they make for a stable, secure society, now as then, so they are very necessary and good.

Now show everyone a very delicate glass vase, which you want to send through the post. Can you just put it in an envelope? (Do so.) Or would tying string round the envelope help? When it is agreed that you will need to pad it to keep it safe, produce some appropriate packaging and ask a couple of people to pack the vase really carefully.

That's what had happened to God's law – because it was so precious to them, people wanted to keep it padded with all sorts of detailed rules, to avoid it getting broken, which is understandable.

But when it's all padded up like this we can't see it and forget what it really looks like. If, when this package arrives, we display it like this on the mantelpiece it isn't going to be much use as a vase any more, is it? The authorities were so fussy about the rule not to carry your mat on the sabbath that they couldn't see that God loves to set us free.

Jesus fulfilled the Law by unwrapping it (do this) so people could once again experience its beauty and use it. (Put some flowers in the vase.) So – we need to keep God's Law and not make excuses about that, but not wrap it up so tightly that we prevent God's glory from being revealed in our loving behaviour, our compassion and our delight in setting people free.

God is our best guide

First ask for an intrepid explorer and blindfold the valiant person who volunteers. Now set out an obstacle course which ends with building a tower of three cartons. The course might have chairs to block the way, something to go under or over and the three cartons at the far end, which are to be brought through the obstacles one by one.

Ask for three other volunteers and explain to the explorer that s/he can choose any one of these guides to help them build the tower by going through the obstacle course. The first guide is blindfold and has his legs tied together. The second guide can see but can only see the place where the carton tower will be built. The third guide can see and is able to move around wherever she likes. The big question is . . . *which guide will the explorer choose?*

Before the explorer chooses, let everyone tell someone near them which guide they would choose and why. Then ask the explorer to decide, and set them off, timing their task to create urgency.

Afterwards explain how God is like the guide who can see and move anywhere he likes. This makes him by far the wisest choice in our lives, because he can see the whole situation, he knows where we are and what our limitations and weaknesses are. He can come alongside us and help us through even the most frightening, or difficult times in our lives.

Rainbows and promises

Beforehand prepare this puzzle for projection on a screen, or on a large display sheet of paper. Alternatively the puzzle can be reproduced on the handout and given to everyone as they come in.

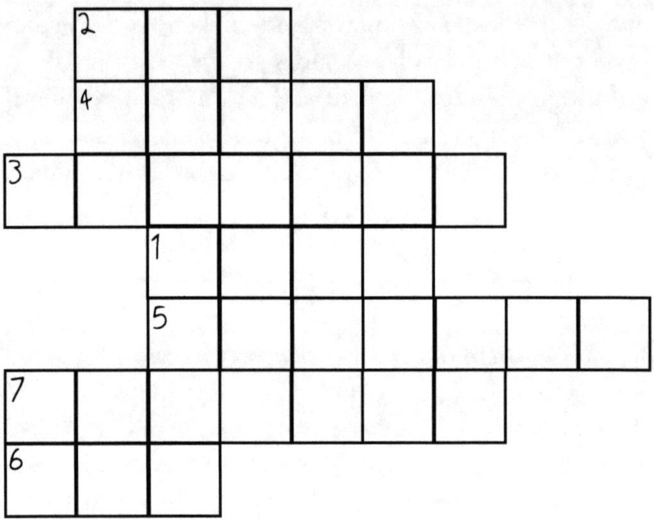

Today's talk will be interspersed with clues to the puzzle. The order of solving the clues is important.

1. *(For a Brownie/Cub/Junior to answer.)*
   Who did God tell to build a large boat?
   As you write in the answer, remind everyone of the wickedness of the people, and God's decision to clean things up, keeping Noah and his family safe because Noah was not doing what everyone else did, but doing what he knew was right in God's eyes.

2. *(For a Mum/Dad/Uncle/Auntie to answer.)*
   What was Noah's boat called?
   As you write the answer, you can tell them that another place this word is used is for the basket Moses was put in when he was a baby. The same people may be able to think of what these two events have in common.

3. *(For anyone under seven.)*
   What did Noah take into the ark with him?
   (They may well say particular sorts of animals. This is fine.) When you've had a few suggestions, and if no one has yet said animals, just gather the ideas together and write in 'animals' to cover them all.

4. *(For Grandads/Grandmas/anyone eligible for a pension.)*
   What did the ark float on?
   Point out how the very water which destroyed everything evil kept Noah, his family and the animals safe.

5. *(For clever people to answer.)*
   When else in the Bible do we find water used as a sign that an old, bad life is being drowned, and yet through this drowning, a person's life is saved?
   Explain that all baptisms used to involve getting totally wet, and that helps us understand the symbol of water. When we are baptised in the name of Jesus, all our previous sin is drowned and destroyed. As we come up out of the water, we are born to a completely new life in Jesus.

6. *(For anyone who ate toast for breakfast.)*
   What was the word you said before 'life in Jesus'?
   If no one gets this first time, repeat the previous sentence about being born into a new life in Jesus. Obviously no one was listening the first time! Explain how this new life is a free gift to us, and we can't ever earn it. What we do have to do is receive it and use it.

7. *(For anyone who came to church on wheels.)*
   When God makes one of these he always keeps it. What is it?
   When Noah and the animals were safe, God made a promise that he would never destroy the earth. As a sign of this promise he used . . . (direct everyone's attention to the vertical word) . . . the rainbow. Whenever we see a rainbow we can remember God's promise to take care of us.

Following God's instructions

First ask for five volunteers and choose people who have curly hair. Tell the congregation that you are going to commission them. Quietly tell the volunteers to go out into the congregation and each collect one person with curly hair and bring them back to you. When they arrive give each person one of these words, written large enough for everyone to read: I AM SENDING YOU OUT AS SHEEP AMONG HUNGRY WOLVES. Ask people in the congregation to unscramble the words and the people to arrange themselves in order. Point out that if the volunteers hadn't obeyed the instructions, the message you wanted to tell everyone would have been incomplete. Added to which they all look a bit like sheep because they all have curly hair!

The original volunteers heard you asking for help because they were paying attention and listening. When God chooses us and commissions us to do something in our life, we will only notice his call if we are paying attention to him and expecting him to communicate with us.

(Write on a flip chart or project on a screen: 1. Pay attention and listen.) Those volunteers stuck to their instructions, even though some people they asked didn't want to go with them. We are to stick to what God asks us to do even if it looks as though our own ideas might get quicker results. (Write or project: 2. Stick to the instructions.)

Our message is a warning to everyone God sends to do his work – it may well be dangerous, hostile and frightening at times to be an active Christian. God very thoughtfully warns us first so that we aren't thrown by this when it happens. (Write or project: 3. Be prepared for big trouble.)

Thank the helpers and display the message.

Living as God designed us

Have an example or two of using something for what it was designed (such as a bicycle being carefully ridden or a sleeping bag to snuggle up in). Have volunteers to demonstrate the correct use of these things.

Now ask people to suggest to the person sitting near them what might happen if we used the bike to iron a shirt or the sleeping bag to skip with. Ask some stalwart volunteers to demonstrate, using a fairly old shirt and tatty sleeping bag in case of accidents.

Explain how God has designed us for living in a certain way – with God at the centre of our lives, caring for one another, being unselfish and respecting each other and one another's property – and it doesn't work very well if we live spiteful, greedy or selfish lives instead. We need to pray every day, keeping closely in touch with God who made us and knows us well, so that we can live out our lives the way he designed us to. That way we'll feel right and our lives will be a lot more useful and cause a lot less damage.

Jesus our Lord

God in the ordinary

Tell everyone that you are about to show them some vitamin B and some energy, some life-giving essence and some potential penicillin. Have a drum roll or dramatic chords on the organ as you whip out of a supermarket bag a loaf of bread.

But this is just an ordinary loaf of bread – how can something so natural and ordinary be all that clever, invisible, scientific stuff? Well, it is! If we were really hungry we could try it and find out how much better it made our bodies feel. (A hungry person can do this.) We eat our way through loaves and loaves of bread every day because we have found that it does us so much good and comes in a form we can easily take naturally – by eating!

So bread is the visible form of all kinds of goodness and life-giving nourishment. And when Jesus talked of himself being the Bread of Life (see John 6:35), he was describing how he is the invisible God in visible form – in the familiar shape of a human being, who we can talk to, watch, touch and listen to.

So why couldn't the religious leaders understand? Why did they find it offensive that Jesus said this?

- Jesus seemed too normal and familiar – they knew him as their carpenter.
- They thought the Son of God should look greater than Moses.
- Their expectations blinded them to seeing the very person they had been waiting generations to meet, when he was standing there right in front of their eyes.

We too need to make sure we don't miss God in the ordinary. In fact, God made everything, so nothing is just ordinary and God can speak to us through his creation, as long as we are ready to notice and listen. Here are some examples.

We often see heavy rain, but usually just moan about it spoiling our hair or stopping a match. Suppose we start actually looking at it and seeing there a picture of how generous and fulsome God is; so many individual droplets of rain – or petals in a tree full of blossom!

Or think of the wide night sky describing God's overarching love; the regular days, nights and seasons showing his faithfulness.

In a dog's dogginess and a young child's openness we can see God showing us the importance of being honestly ourselves; when we see weeds and wild flowers growing over a rubbish dump we see God telling us about redemption, and how everything can be made new and beautiful.

All we need to do is train our spiritual eyes to look, so that we don't miss out on anything God is wanting to say to us, even through the ordinary things.

Jesus is baptised

Ask various children if they know what job they would like to do when they grow up. Ask various adults what they wanted to be when they were children, and whether they did it or not. Ask some of the children if they have seen pictures of their mums and dads when they were babies and toddlers. Do they look anything like that now? Ask some of the mums and dads if they can imagine what their children will be like in twenty years' time.

Now let's look at Jesus (see Matthew 3:13-17). Here he is at about thirty years old. He's a carpenter, so he's probably quite strongly built. He's heard that his cousin, John (do they remember John?), is washing people in the River Jordan as a sign that God has forgiven their sins. We wash to get our bodies clean. John baptised people to show they were getting their souls clean. They were all getting ready for the Messiah, or Christ.

And now here comes Jesus, wading into the river, and wanting John to baptise him as well! (We know that Jesus is the Christ they were waiting for, but the people didn't know that yet.) John realises who Jesus is, and is shocked that he wants to be baptised. 'It ought to be the other way round!' says John. '*You* ought to be baptising *me!*'

Jesus insists. 'No, it's right for you to baptise me. God's work of putting things right all through the centuries is coming together now in this Baptism.' So John agrees to baptise Jesus. He pushes Jesus down under the water in the river, and when Jesus comes up out of the water, something amazing happens.

It's as if the heavens are opened up, and Jesus sees the Spirit of God coming to him and resting on him. Matthew tells us it looked something like a dove flying down to him. Jesus hears God his Father speaking to him deep into his being. God is saying that Jesus is indeed his well-loved Son, chosen and marked out for a special life that will save the world.

So that tiny baby, born in the stable, visited by shepherds and wise men, looked after by Joseph and Mary all through his childhood, is now at the start of his important work on earth. His job is to show the world God's love.

Jesus fufils the prophets

Prepare this crossword puzzle on a large sheet of card.

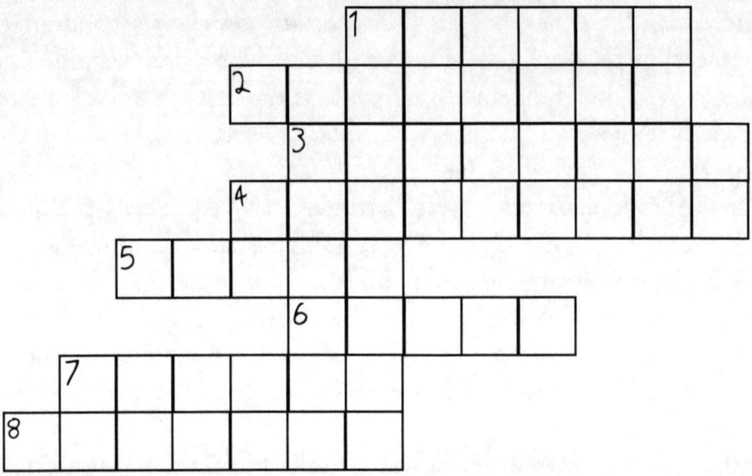

Give out each clue in turn; I have suggested who to allow to answer each one but do of course change this to suit the group. Make sure that everyone present has a chance to answer at least one clue.

Across:

1. *(For uniformed people only)*
   The plural of person.
2. *(For those with long hair only)*
   To say what will happen in the future.
3. *(For those with short hair only)*
   Truthfully.
4. *(For those wearing green)*
   Special and significant.
5. *(For those with brown eyes)*
   The real facts about something.
6. *(For those without brown eyes)*
   The name of Mary and Joseph's son.
7. *(For those who like pizza)*
   Christmas without the last three letters.
8. *(For those who can/could skip)*
   Fills with meaning; manages to accomplish something.

Down:

1. *(Everybody)*
   The hidden word in this puzzle.
   Solution to 1 down: PROPHETS

Now ask everyone to help you with your sermon notes by calling out the words as you point to them. Read the message so that everyone joins in at the right places, like this:

PROPHETS are PEOPLE. False PROPHETS FORETELL what PEOPLE are wanting to hear, but good PROPHETS FORETELL HONESTLY IMPORTANT TRUTH from God. To FORETELL doesn't just mean to FORETELL the future, it can also mean to speak out God's TRUTH even when PEOPLE don't want to hear it. JESUS CHRIST FULFILS the IMPORTANT TRUTH about God which the good PROPHETS were able to FORETELL HONESTLY. In everything JESUS does, both during his time on earth and ever since through PEOPLE who believe in him, JESUS shows the IMPORTANT TRUTH about God's love for PEOPLE. So who are PROPHETS? PROPHETS are PEOPLE who FORETELL HONESTLY IMPORTANT TRUTH from God, and JESUS CHRIST FULFILS it.

Clothed in humanity

Beforehand cut out a simple white cloth tunic like this to fit a three- or four-year-old.

Invite a couple of toddlers and their parents to the front and interview them about the coats or jackets the children are wearing. Admire them and ask where they were bought, and what size was needed compared with their last coat.

Tell everyone how Samuel was brought to the temple when he was able to feed himself, and every year his mum brought him a new linen coat she had made (see 1 Samuel 2:18,19). Every year he needed a slightly bigger one as he grew older. Produce your linen ephod lookalike and dress the toddler in it. As you do so, explain that it was worn as a sign of coming before God with a clean heart and mind. Priests all wore them, too.

When God came to earth as a baby, it was like him putting on the clothing of being human, and it was God's way of showing how much he loves us and is with us. It also helps us to see what God is like, because we cannot see God, but in Jesus we can see how God behaves. We can see that he enjoys people's company, wants to help them and shares their sadness and joy.

And Jesus didn't suddenly arrive on earth as a grown-up. He was born as a baby (draw attention to the size of someone very small in the congregation) and grew to be a toddler and a child (use other people of appropriate ages to demonstrate), so by the time he was a grown-up twelve-year-old he had experienced all the sort of human things that we experience.

Use the larger tunic with the word 'Humanity' written on it to clothe a twelve(ish)-year-old. All twelve-year-olds start asking questions about God and themselves, and so did Jesus. Part of wearing humanity meant that he developed as a human person and now he was grown-up he was fascinated to know who he was and why he was alive, just as we are. Those questions are important, and need to be asked. They are a sign of growing up. The answers for Jesus (and the answers for us) didn't come all at once. But his visit to the temple when he was twelve (see Luke 2:41-52) seems to have been a very important one for him. He began to understand that he was on earth to carry out God's purposes. That was why he was wearing the clothing of humanity. Perhaps for some of us, today is an important time for finding out God's purpose for us in our lives. We need to come into God's presence wearing the clothes of honesty and openness, and ask our questions.

Transfiguration

Bring along a family photograph album with snaps of holidays or celebrations in it, and if possible a camera which takes instant pictures. Also have two cards to hold up, one with a large plus sign on and the other a large minus sign.

If you have an instant camera, begin by taking a picture of some people or the day's flower arrangement. Show the album and talk about the way we all like to snap away to capture the moments when we are on holiday or at a special celebration, or when our children and grandchildren are growing up. We want to hang on to the moment and cherish it for years to come, because we know the moment itself won't last. The children will soon grow up, and we may never have the chance to visit the Eiffel Tower or Southend illuminations ever again!

The 'plus' side of taking pictures like this (encourage everyone's suggestions) may be that we will remember better if we look back at the picture – it may help us see the importance of the occasion, it helps us pass on the family tradition to the next generation, and it lets us enjoy more at our leisure later than we were able to take in at the time.

The 'minus' side may be that we're so busy taking pictures at the time that we aren't able to concentrate properly on the actual moment.

In Matthew 17:1-9 we hear about something amazing which happened on a mountain in Galilee. Three of Jesus' friends – Peter, James and John – saw Jesus shining with God's glory as he prayed. It was one of those times when Peter wanted to reach for the camera (except that cameras hadn't been invented then) so they could hold on to the wonderful moment for ever. Perhaps they had never before felt God quite so close to them! They even heard God's voice. He wasn't saying, 'I hope you're watching carefully and I'm sorry cameras haven't been invented yet or you could have got a pretty dramatic picture here today!' He was helping them understand the real, actual experience they were in, assuring them that Jesus really was God's Son, and wanting them to listen to Jesus in a way they had never listened before.

God doesn't just want Peter, James and John to know – he wants St Peter's church and St James's and St John's and all the other churches to know. He wants all the people in all the world to know who Jesus is, and he wants us all to pay attention to what Jesus says, and really listen to him with our hearts and minds as well as our ears.

God's loving risk

First ask for a couple of volunteers to start balloons off from the back of the church and ask everyone to try to pass these balloons up across the seats to the front without letting them drop to the floor or go backwards.

Then talk about how it feels to start at the bottom again when you change schools, go to a different area or have to change your job after being made redundant. Rather like the balloons, you feel a bit wobbly and vulnerable, and are not sure if you'll be able to manage.

Jesus, the Word, or expression of God, had been present when our universe first began. He knew all about the excitement of stars bursting into being, planets being formed and all the ideas of creation taking shape. But so as to put us right and give us life that wouldn't end, he was quite prepared to put all that aside and become a human baby, starting at the weakest level. God was willing to become one of the creatures he had made.

It was bound to be a very dangerous journey, because he was depending on people, and people can let you down. People can be dangerous, people can kill. (Pop the balloons.) God knew the risk he was taking, but because he loved us he reckoned we were worth the risk. The worst happened, and some people hated the goodness and love they saw in Jesus. Jesus allowed himself to be killed, but death couldn't hold the God of life. He came to life again having won the terrible battle against evil for us. He will be alive now for ever, reigning over us, loving us and living both in heaven and in our lives when we let him in.

Which is easier?

Start by explaining that you have a list of hard things to do, and you are going to ask everyone which they think is easiest of two options. They can have a moment to think or confer, and then a show of hands should indicate their communal decision.
Here are the options:

1. Learning to ride a bike, or learning to talk.
2. Earning money, or saving your money up without spending any.
3. Doing something brave, or doing something thoughtful.
4. Talking non-stop for an hour, or being completely quiet for an hour.

In Mark 2:1-12 Jesus asks a similar question. Remind them of the circumstances – the crowds, the paralysed man let down through the roof, Jesus telling him his sins are forgiven, and the scribes, knowing that only God can forgive sins, horrified that Jesus has done what only God can do. This was his question – which is it easier to say to the paralysed man: 'Your sins are forgiven you' or 'Stand up, take your bed and walk'?

Let's try and work out an answer. First we need to make a few things clear. Who is the only one who can forgive sins? It's God. And what about a paralysed man suddenly being able to get up and walk home – who's the only one able to do that? Once again, it's God. So in a way Jesus is saying to the scribes, 'Is it easier for me to act like God, or to act like God?' And what would be the answer to that? There'd be no difference; both are a natural way for God to behave.

The man's body was paralysed – that meant he couldn't make it move freely. When Jesus healed him he was free to move about again. It's like that when our lives are jammed by sin and guilt about bad things we've done in the past. When God forgives us completely, he unjams us, so we are free to live happily again.

The Resurrection

Beforehand cut a rough circle shape from a very large carton (such as will hide a small child). This represents a gravestone. Also cut a number of teardrop shapes out of paper and leave one of these on each row before the service. Just before the talk secrete a small child behind the card gravestone, holding a bunch of spring flowers.

First talk about times when we have been disappointed with a present or a treat, and how let down and rather flat we feel. The disciples must have felt like that on Good Friday when Jesus, their master and friend had been killed.

Sometimes we feel disappointed with God, too. Perhaps he doesn't answer our prayer for someone we love to get better, or perhaps things aren't working out for us in the way we hoped they would. Ask people to find the teardrop on their row and, as they pass it along to the aisle, to look at it and think of their own personal disappointments or regrets. Have a couple of people to collect the teardrops in a basket and walk up in silence to lay them at the foot of the cross. In a way, that's what was happening as Jesus hung dying there.

But Jesus couldn't be bound in death, and on the third day the cave entrance was found rolled away and Jesus was alive. At this point, roll the card stone away and the small child jumps up, holding a bunch of flowers, which s/he gives out to people all over the church.

Jesus shows us God

You will need a supermarket bag and two or three things in it which have distinctive shapes (such as a squash/wine bottle, a banana and a saucepan).

Show everyone the bag and ask them what they think might be inside. It might be all sorts of things, but we don't know because we can't see them. That's what a lot of people think about God – he might be there but they don't know because they haven't seen him.

Suppose I let someone come and feel the things in the bag. (Invite someone to do so.) Now they are getting some experience of what the things feel like, and that gives them a much better idea of what they are. All through the Old Testament people groped their way to understanding what God was like, and they felt his presence with them as they were led out of slavery in Egypt.

Suppose I show you the things in this bag? (Take the objects out and display them so everyone can see.) A couple of thousand years ago, God came physically into our world and walked around as a human person. His name was Jesus and at last everyone could see exactly what God was like.

Suppose I put the things back out of sight again. Do you still know what they are and what they are like? Yes, we know for certain because we have seen them. When we say that we believe Jesus is alive, it doesn't mean that we think he might be – it means we know for certain that he is because we have seen him in the gospels, we've seen him in the way his close friends live, and we've met him in our own lives and felt his closeness to us. Our faith is not about a list of rules, but about a real, living person who can completely transform our lives.

Seeing what God is like

Ask a volunteer to stand at the front, holding a large piece of card in front of them so that no one can see their face. Point out that we can't be certain whether the person is looking happy, sad or angry, because we can't see for ourselves. Ask the volunteer to make one of those expressions behind the card. We can talk to them and listen to them, but we can't see them. It was a little like that for the people of Israel. Sometimes the prophets would speak out God's word to them, and they prayed to God, but it wasn't until Jesus came that people could see what God was like.

(Take the card from the volunteer's face.) We can now see clearly whether the person is happy, sad or angry, and we can see how s/he behaves, and what s/he thinks is important. When Jesus came to live as a human being on our earth, walking about in the actual place of Galilee and in the actual time of Roman-occupied Palestine, people could see exactly what God thought was important, and how much he loved them.

They saw that God really is interested in our everyday worries such as having enough food, or enough time or energy to get our work done.

They saw that God goes on loving us right to the very limit and still carries on loving! (Jesus went on loving and forgiving right through being put to death on a cross.)

They saw that God likes to work with us in solving some of our problems, and, if we are happy to work with him, amazing things can happen.

There will be lots of times this week when we can choose to do 'exactly what Jesus tells us' and, if we agree, God will be able to use us in providing lovingly for someone's needs. Perhaps we will be giving our complete attention to someone when they talk to us, or providing financial help or emotional support. Perhaps our smile will cheer someone up, or our help will give someone a well-needed rest. Perhaps by letting someone play we will be making them feel less lonely and happier. Perhaps the spare curtains we remember to take into the charity shop will be exactly what someone is hoping to find as they struggle to furnish a home with very little money.

Let's make sure that this week we listen out for the ways God asks for our help, and then do what he whispers in our hearts, so that the people in this town can actually see God's love in action.

Shine, Jesus, shine

Bring along something that gets transformed when the light in it is switched on, such as an illuminated globe or table lamp. Or people can look at the church's stained glass windows.

First show it without being lit up, and then switch on to show the difference. When it is lit up we can see patterns and colours that we may not have seen before. In Mark 9:2-9 we are told about a time when three of Jesus' friends saw him 'lit up', and it really did help them to see him in a new light.

We're none of us used to that kind of thing happening, so it all sounds rather strange to us. Let's imagine ourselves that morning, climbing up a steep, rocky mountain path with Jesus leading the way, and Peter, James and John struggling to keep up behind him. We're all panting a bit, and sometimes pieces of stone and grit get stuck in our sandals. We might see a lizard or two sitting in the early sun, and hear the wind in the grass.

When we reach the very top, we can see all around us, with the lake and the little villages far below. It's like being on top of the world. Jesus has come up here to pray. He knows that he needs to get away from the crowds sometimes to spend time quietly with his Father in heaven. We all need that, too.

Peter, James and John suddenly realise that Jesus is looking different. He seems to be shining – Mark says 'dazzling' which is like when you look into the sun and have to screw up your eyes because it's just too bright to look at comfortably. It's as if they're looking at the presence of God himself, here on the mountain. And Jesus isn't alone, either. As if he's in heaven, rather than standing on the mountain grass, two other people are talking with him, and we recognise them from history. One is Moses, who led the people out of slavery in Egypt and gave the people God's ten commandments, and the other is a prophet from long ago called Elijah; both very holy people.

It's actually very frightening – all so holy and full of glory, and so unusual. It's then that the cloud comes over, and I think Peter, James and John have shielded their eyes from all the brightness. They hear a voice speaking out of the cloud, and they somehow know that it is God speaking. What is it he's saying? 'This is my beloved Son: listen to him.'

That's Jesus he's talking about! And we've just seen with our own eyes that Jesus wears God's glory – we just haven't been allowed to notice it before.

When the disciples look up again the brightness has passed, and their friend Jesus is standing there on his own, looking quite normal. On the way down the mountain path he tells them not to say anything about what they have seen and shared until he has risen from the dead. Peter, James and John don't really understand yet that Jesus will have to suffer death before he is glorified.

But we know what happened, don't we? And perhaps it helped Jesus' friends, when the first Easter Day came, and they met Jesus alive again that evening, to see how God had been glorified even in the dark sadness of the cross, because even there Jesus had been shining with love for us all.

Goodbye?

Begin by talking about saying goodbye. The kind of goodbye it is depends on how well we know each other, whether we love or hate each other, and whether we are saying goodbye for a short time, a long time or for ever. In Acts 1:6-11 we see the disciples as Jesus says goodbye to them. Since Easter he had been meeting up with them after the Resurrection. Sometimes he had met them when they were all together, sometimes on their own. They would suddenly recognise him, or he would suddenly be there among them, and the disciples had begun to get used to Jesus being with them even when they couldn't see him with their eyes.

Now, here they are, all together with Jesus, and this is going to be their last goodbye to him as a person whom they see with their eyes, because he is going back to heaven. He tells them two things: (show a picture of rushing wind and flames) that they are going to be given power when the Holy Spirit comes upon them, and (show a picture of an empty speech bubble) that they are going to tell lots of people all over the world about the Jesus they know and love so well.

Then we are told that he was lifted up, while they watched, and a cloud took him from their sight so that they couldn't see him any more. So they stood there, peering up into the sky, rather like you do when you've just let a balloon go, and you watch and watch until you can't see it any more. What happened next?

They realised that two people, dressed in white, were standing next to them. 'Why are you standing here looking up into the sky?' they asked. They told the disciples that one day Jesus would come in the same way they had seen him go. But what they wanted them to know was that there wasn't any point in hanging around in that one place for a glimpse of Jesus, because he had gone on to the next phase, where he would be with all his friends, including us, all the time, not in a way that we can see, but in new ways. Just as real, just as much alive, but in a form which makes him free to be in all kinds of different countries and places and dates and times all at once!

What he said to the disciples that day, he says to us as well: we will be given power when the Holy Spirit comes upon us (show the first picture again) and we are going to tell lots of people about the Jesus we know and love (show the second picture).

Jesus our Saviour

Jesus to the rescue

If you have a member of the congregation whose job involves rescue (for example in the fire, ambulance, lifeboat or mountain rescue services), ask if they would be willing to take part in a brief interview before the talk. Talk with them about the kind of dangers they themselves have to accept in order to rescue people, and the way they get alongside the people who need rescuing in order to help them. If you are not having a live interview, talk briefly about these rescuers.

Explain how Jesus is a rescuer, who comes in person to save us and help us. Stand someone on a paper island in the middle of a flood. God doesn't stand a long way off and shout to us. (Stand a long way off and shout to them to get into a boat and sail away.) That's no good, because the person feeling drowned by sadness or guilt or evil can't do what you are shouting even if they wanted to. We can't rescue ourselves; only God can set us free by accepting us, loving us and forgiving us. So instead of being a long way off and telling us what to do, God came in person to rescue us. (Pretend to row over to the person and then rescue them.) That's what happened at the first Christmas – God came to live among us in the person of Jesus, and he is still with us now. We are all his brothers and sisters.

Resisting temptation

On matching sets of three graded sizes of card, from A5 to huge, write these two messages, with the print and thickness increasing with the card size.

I want it and I want it now.

Love God and love one another.

Begin by explaining that Jesus went into the desert after he had been baptised, and had a very hard time out there being tempted (see Luke 4:1-13). We all know what it feels like to be tempted. It's when we want something or want to do something which we know is wrong. (Show the middle-sized 'I want it and I want it now' card.) Ask someone to hold this card, but don't make them stand with their arms in the air for ages.

Jesus was being tempted to turn the stones into bread so he could eat them, but he knew that this would be using his power in a selfish way. He remembered that he loved God and he loved other people (display the largest 'Love God and love one another' sign). Ask someone else to hold this up.

As you can see, the love for God and other people stayed bigger than the temptation, and so Jesus was able to stand firm and not let the temptation get the better of him.

Whenever Jesus was tempted he always remembered that his love for God and other people was much stronger than the 'I want'. Put these signs down.

Now let's see what happens with us. First we get a little temptation inside us. (Give one helper the smallest 'I want' sign.) It isn't very big and we remember the right way to live (give the other helper the middle-sized 'Love God' sign) so we don't give way to the temptation.

But as we think about it more, this happens. (Exchange the small 'I want' for the middle-sized one.) And now there's a battle going on inside us, because the 'I want' is the same size as the 'Love God'. If we're not careful the 'I want' will get even bigger! (Swap it for the largest 'I want' sign.) And when we let the 'I want' get bigger than the 'Love God', even for a minute, we're in danger of falling into temptation, and doing or saying what we really know is wrong.

Jesus shows us how to do this. As soon as you feel a little 'I want' coming on (show it), remember that you love God and you love other people more than you want what is wrong. (Display the middle-sized 'Love God' sign.) And if the 'I want' gets bigger in you (show the middle-sized 'I want') think hard about how you and God love each other (show the largest 'Love God' sign) so that the 'I want' is less strong and you can fight it; and instead of giving in and doing or saying what you know is wrong, God will be helping you to stand up to temptation and win.

Who is Jesus?

Beforehand, ask a few people of different ages to provide you with a photograph of them when they were very young, and have these pictures duplicated, or shown on a screen. Don't identify them, but say they are all members of the church community. When people have had a go at guessing the identities, ask the people to come to the front. This narrows the choice, and makes it easier to see who's who. We might have a hunch about someone, and can ask them directly. They will tell us whether or not we are right, and then we'll know for certain. (Invite people to do this.) Once we know the true identity, it's often easier to see the likeness!

Jesus knew that people had all sorts of ideas about who he was (see Matthew 16:13-17). Some ideas were close to the truth, some were wide of the mark, and Jesus always wanted his followers to make the discovery for themselves. Discovering something for ourselves means that we always remember it far better than when we have simply been told things. (People may remember discovering for themselves that fire burns, for instance, that cement hardens into a solid lump, or that overloading a computer can cause it to crash.)

No doubt Jesus sensed that the disciples had almost got to the point of discovering that he was not just their friend and teacher, but also the promised Messiah, the Son of God. This conversation, starting with what other people think, will help them tip over into that 'Aha!' of learning, that point when you suddenly know something and everything falls clearly into place.

It is Simon, the fisherman, who comes out with it for the first time. 'You are the Christ,' he says, 'the Son of the living God.' It must have been a bit like when you first say the words 'I love you' or 'I'm three'. It's the first time you have ever said it and as you say it, you know it is really true, and your life will never be quite the same again.

The Bread of Life

Ask who had a meal yesterday, and express surprise that they are thinking of having another meal today – some have already eaten today and are still planning to eat lunch! They can explain to you that our bodies need food every day for them to stay strong and healthy, and for the children to grow. We run on food like a car runs on petrol.

Produce a loaf of bread. Remind everyone of how Jesus had fed all those people with enough bread and fish, and they had all enjoyed their meal (see John 6:24-35). Now they are all running after Jesus the next day as well. Some of them want to hear what Jesus says, some want to come and be healed, some want to come because it's exciting going where everyone else is going and they don't want to miss out on anything. And lots are going because they remember those nice tuna sandwiches – the meal they ate with Jesus.

Why does Jesus want them to have come? Collect various ideas, and draw out that Jesus wants them to be there because they know they will meet with God if they're with Jesus.

But Jesus knows all too well why some of them have really come, and he tells them so – 'You're looking for me because you ate the bread and were satisfied.'

And then he helps them to understand how God feeds us not just with bread for our bodies, while we live on this earth for seventy years or so (keep holding the bread), but in another way as well. He gives us spiritual food which keeps us alive through this life and right on into life beyond physical death. With that feeding we won't be finishing as soon as we die, but going on living for ever.

The people thought that sounded pretty good bread to have, and asked Jesus if he would give them some, so they could be fed spiritually as well as physically. And Jesus told them (lift the loaf of bread up high), 'I am the Bread of Life!' So it's Jesus himself who we feed on.

What does that mean? Obviously we're not like cannibals, eating Jesus up – he didn't mean that. But if we think how satisfied we feel when we have been very hungry and then eat a good meal, that's how our spirits feel when we spend time with Jesus – contented and satisfied, happy and full of energy and health. And just as we need to keep eating ordinary food every day, so we need to keep spending time with Jesus every day, so that, spiritually as well as physically, we will be growing strong and healthy, and we'll stay that way even when our physical bodies get old and weak, and when they stop working so that we die. Even then we'll be spiritually bounding with life and energy, ready to spend eternity alive in God's company.

The Water of Life

You will need some paper cups, one with holes poked in it, a washing-up bowl or bucket and a jug of water.

Remind everyone of the way the people in the desert were very thirsty, and Moses asked God how their thirst could be quenched (see Exodus 17:1-7). He also told God how grumpy everyone was getting – they were so grumpy that Moses began to think they might take their anger out on him physically! God answered by providing water tumbling out of a rock, fresh and pure and delicious. There's nothing more wonderful when you're thirsty than the refreshing sound and taste of water. Now pour some water out and enjoy the sound of it. Invite some thirsty person to drink some from the proper cup. The people wanted to be back in the past, but God wanted to lead them on into the future.

John 4:5-15 tells us about two more water supplies. One was a well, where a woman had come to collect water, and where Jesus was sitting, feeling thirsty. Perhaps his own thirst reminded him of the people getting grumpy with Moses in the desert, and the way God had given them the flowing, living water they needed.

The other water supply is a bit unusual. Jesus told the woman about some water which would quench her thirst completely, and become a spring of water inside her welling up to give her life that lasts for ever. At first the woman thought this sounded too good to be true! What Jesus was doing was explaining the way God fills our lives, and leads us into the future, satisfying us all the way along, and refreshing us when we are sad and longing for good and right and fair and helpful things to happen in our world. The more we go to God to be filled with his living water of life and love, the more we shall find that we too are becoming sources of love and comfort and fairness and truthfulness for other people.

Let's see what happens when we pour some water into this cup with holes in it. (Station some people around with proper cups.) Pretend this hol(e)y cup is a Christian drinking the living water of life and love from the living, loving God. Can you see how the Christian then pours out that love to other people he or she meets? There's no problem that God will suddenly dry up, because God is living, flowing, for ever. And the other people may well want to become hol(e)y themselves, drinking that eternal supply which they can see is changing us for the better.

So if your life feels rather dry or thirsty or stuck in the past, go to Jesus; keep going to Jesus; and let him fill you up with the living spiritual water that really satisfies. And don't keep it all to yourself – pass it on!

The sheep-door

Using chairs, build a circular sheepfold, with a gap for the entrance. Ask for some volunteer sheep to go inside. Explain that this is what a sheepfold was like in Jesus' day, except that it was made of stones, not chairs. Is there a door? No, there isn't. That's because the shepherd himself was the door. Ask a volunteer shepherd to come and be the door of the sheepfold. (You could even give the shepherd a stick or crook from the Nativity costumes, and a shepherd's sling.) Why is this living door likely to be a good safe one for the sheep? Because the shepherd would hear any dangers, such as wolves, or bears, or sheep stealers, and take action to protect the sheep, using his staff or sling. (The shepherd can pretend to frighten off a dangerous wolf.)

Another thing about sheep is that they get very frightened by lots of things, but when they hear the voice of the shepherd at the door they know they can trust him, and they feel safe. They will even follow him when he calls them and leads them off to some good juicy grass. (The sheep can try this.) And then they will follow the shepherd back home at the end of the day. (They do this.)

Now why are we getting a lesson in sheep farming this morning? What has all this got to do with Jesus? Or us?

In John 10:7-15 we hear Jesus telling the people that he is the sheep-door. (And you know what that means, now.) He told them all about the sheep being safe when the shepherd is the door, and the sheep knowing the shepherd's voice and following him. (You know about that too.) But the people didn't have a clue why Jesus was talking to them about sheep and shepherds. So they asked him to explain.

Jesus said he was trying to tell them something important about God. (Can anyone think what it was?) He was telling the people that they were a bit like sheep and Jesus was like the good shepherd who lies down in the doorway to keep the sheep safe. He was saying that God looks after us and defends us with his life because he loves us so much. He hates the thought of us coming to harm, and fights off evil. We can trust God's voice when he calls us, and follow him without any fear because we know God is always faithful and good and loving.

So whenever you are scared to face a bad problem, or bad ideas and temptations keep coming at you, stand there in the sheepfold behind Jesus, the sheep-door, and you will be safe. And whenever you are muddled about whether to do something or not, or whether to be selfish or not, listen out for the quiet calling of the Good Shepherd (you won't hear it with your ears, but you will know it in yourself) and follow him into the way that is right and good and kind and loving.

The Good Shepherd

Gather all the young children in the aisle and get them doing sheepy things like eating grass, drinking from a stream, sitting and chewing, and bleating. Place a few older children around the edges of the building to be wolves and bears, sheep-watching and hoping for a chance to eat one of the lambs. They can howl sadly as they wait, or growl. One person is a good shepherd, keeping an eye on the flock, and watching out for any signs of wolves and bears.

The wild animals are waiting for the shepherd to go for a break, or doze off, because that's when they might get a chance to grab a lamb or sheep. But this shepherd loves his sheep, and that means he isn't going to give the wild animals any opportunity to attack the flock. He's ready to defend them with his life, if necessary.

Now swap the shepherd for a hired hand. Here's a different flock, with a different shepherd, further up the valley. The wild animals have gathered here now, and they're still waiting. (Howls and growls). A couple of wolves start to come closer, but this shepherd doesn't frighten them away – he just runs away! The wolves get more confident. They're getting dangerously close, and the sheep are all huddled together, when that good shepherd walks up, with stones in his catapult, and the wolves back off quick!

Thank the sheep and wild animals for their help, and explain that Jesus is like a good shepherd, who cares for us and looks after us, protecting us from evil. He loves us, so he isn't going to let us down, and is even ready to lay down his life for his sheep (see John 10:11-16). In fact, as we know, Jesus did just that – he was ready to lay down his life to set us free.

The grapevine

Cut six long strips of green crepe paper, or lengths of green string. Also prepare ten cut-out bunches of grapes from coloured paper.

Begin by suggesting that if you came in and said you were a pair of curtains, everyone would probably tell you to pull yourself together. But in John 15:1-8 we find Jesus saying, 'I am a grapevine.' Obviously he wasn't really a grapevine, was he? So what on earth did he mean?

To help us understand, we're going to make a kind of grapevine. Ask one volunteer to hold a green string in each hand, and two others to tie the strings round their waists. They can now hold four strings between them, and four others can tie these round their waists. Now for the fruit. Each of the last four people can hold a bunch of grapes in each hand (eight altogether) and the other two bunches can be stuck with a loop of sticky tape to the fronts of the second two volunteers.

In just a short time, and with just a few people, we've grown quite a big vine and ten bunches of fruit! Just imagine how much fruit there would be if everyone here was joined on the vine.

Jesus said he was the true vine and his Father was the gardener, looking after the growing and helping the vine branches to produce as much fruit as possible. Obviously these branches are only able to produce their fruit if they're joined on to the vine, because all the life-giving sap feeds them and if they're cut off they don't get anything to keep them alive.

Jesus was really saying that if we want our lives to produce fruit like love, joy, peace, patience, kindness, goodness, faithfulness, gentleness and self-control (stick these labels on the grapes), then we have to make really sure that we're joined up to Jesus and in touch with him. We need his life in us all the time. We need to keep in touch with him every day!

Comfort and healing

Begin by asking people to imagine a child who has gone outside to play. She has been learning to ride her bike, and is quite good at it now, with a few wobbles. She's happy out there, riding up and down, until she takes a corner a bit steeply, brakes sharply, and she and the bike crash down. The child has a nasty graze on her leg, and is upset and a bit frightened by the fall. All she can think of is getting back home, to the person she knows will make it all better, and there she is, limping up the road, with her leg bleeding, crying out for her mum as she goes.

Most of us have been there. Whenever we're badly hurt, even when we've grown up, there's a young child inside us limping back home, crying, to the place we feel safe, and to the person we know will look after us and make it all better.

It's a good picture of our loving parent God, who is always there, waiting for his hurt and limping children to walk back home to the one who can and does make it all better, however old or young we are, and however we got our wounds. What that walk back home shows is that the child trusts. What our walk back to God shows is that we know and love and trust God to help us.

In Mark 10:46-52 we meet a blind man called Bartimaeus. He knew he was blind. He knew he missed out in life because he couldn't see. When he heard that Jesus was passing by, he shouted and kept on shouting, so he wouldn't miss his chance. Never mind if the disciples told him to be quiet, he knew this was too important an opportunity to miss, and he shouted hard until Jesus himself heard him. That gave him the chance to do his 'limping home' – he made his way to the person he knew could help him. And, sure enough, Jesus did just that.

Don't panic

If practical, arrange for a couple of people to bring their (well-controlled) pet into church this morning. If this isn't possible, interview a couple of pet owners.

Look at the animals and talk to the owners about what they like to eat, and how they like to play. Then ask them about how their pets behave when they are frightened or feel threatened, and how they calm them down.

It isn't just pets who get worried, angry and upset – it's humans as well. In Mark 4:35-41 we read about a time when Jesus' friends were so frightened they were panicking, and we saw how Jesus calmed them down. Remind them that Jesus was actually asleep, and the disciples woke him up to tell him to start worrying! With the stormy waves pitching the boat up and down, and the water coming in over the side it was beginning to look like a *Titanic* situation, and there was Jesus fast asleep in the bottom of the boat!

Sometimes we do that, too, if life seems very scary, and everything seems to be going wildly out of control. We scream out to Jesus, demanding that he notices and *does* something, instead of being so calm about it all. It's almost as if we want him to panic as well.

Jesus, once he's been thoroughly shaken awake, doesn't seem to be caught up in the excitement. But he can see that it isn't only the disciples who are churned up – it's the weather as well. And perhaps he sees here a good way to help the disciples understand more about who he is. The disciples are so scared at the moment that they can't take anything in. So instead of calming them down, Jesus calms the wind and the waves. As the howling wind eases and settles quietly again, and the pounding waves flatten back to a gentle lapping around the battered boat, the disciples calm down as well. In this lull they recover themselves and stop panicking.

What does Jesus do next – wait for their applause? Go back to sleep? In fact we find he now starts teaching them, because they are now calm enough to listen. He talks to them about trusting God, even in the middle of raging storms.

Often in life we will find that when we have invited Jesus into our boat – into our life – we don't get so thrown by all the stormy problems (things like quarrels in friendships, loved ones moving away, financial problems, pressure and stress at work). And if we're panicking about them so much that we can't hear Jesus helping us to weather the storm, then often we'll find we're given a breather – a bit of space – where things are calmed down long enough for us to realise that, with God in charge, we don't actually need to be terrified.

Stressful lives

Bring along a crowded diary or calendar, and other gadgets for coping with busy lifestyles, such as a computerised notebook, a laptop, mobile phone, alarm clock or fax message.

Ask a few children to walk up and down pretending to be talking on their mobiles or driving their cars, while you talk about the way we can now continue our office work walking along the High Street or on the train. We can send messages by e-mail or fax so that they get there almost immediately. All this enables us to spend more and more of our time being fully at work if we happen to have a job, with increasing pressure and decreasing space in our lives. People have either far too much work than is healthy or none at all, and leisure activities often have to slot in some frantic physical activity to compensate for all the physically inactive work of brain and adrenaline. Advertisements shout at us to buy this, choose that, look like them; the newspapers and magazines advise us what to think and how to behave, and often we believe their lies. We are like a scattered flock of sheep racing in different directions, without knowing where we are or where we are going.

(Stop the children and have them sit down very still wherever they are.)

In Mark 6:30-34 we learn about Jesus' busy ministry of teaching and healing, listening and encouraging. When he and his disciples had been hard at work for days, and were really tired and drained, they'd get into a boat to sail across the lake for a bit of peace and quiet – only to find all the crowds had run round the edge of the lake and were already there waiting for them! Jesus didn't send them away and tell them what the office hours were, or put them on hold. He didn't ask Peter to change course and sail off somewhere else instead.

Instead, Jesus saw the lost and struggling lives, the need for reassurance and practical, wise teaching, the longing for healing and wholeness, and the hearts attracted to God but needing help to find him. And seeing all that, he loved them, with the deep affection of God's love; he climbed wearily out of the boat and fed them with the teaching and comforting they so badly needed. From stories like this of Jesus' ministry we know with certainty that God never ever turns any of us away. None of our needs or wounds or sorrows are hidden from him. Whenever we run around the lake to be there waiting for him, he will step on to our beach and minister to us, because he loves us. Like a good shepherd he is concerned for our well-being and leads us carefully and safely through time into the eternity of heaven.

The Way, the Truth and the Life

Ask two or three experts to come and explain the way they do whatever it is they are good at. (The actual areas of expertise depend on the interests of your congregation, but try and choose people from representative age and interest groups. The skill should be capable of being demonstrated in front of everyone, so it could be ironing, juggling, dribbling a football, doing a cartwheel or skipping, for example.)

First ask each one to explain it to you, placing them out of sight of everyone as they do so. Share with the congregation how it all sounds incredibly complicated, and difficult to follow, even though it is obviously expert advice. That's rather how it is with the Old Testament Law – everyone respects it highly and it's very good advice for living, but somehow we never seem to manage to follow the instructions or get the hang of them. They help us to know how to live a good life, but they don't change us so that we are able to do it. Some of the prophets had told everyone that one day it would be different. People wouldn't need those instructions any more, because they would already know, in their hearts, how to behave properly.

Let's find out if we can understand our experts any better if we can actually see them doing these clever things. (Invite them to demonstrate, one by one.) Ah, that's much clearer! We may not be able to do it ourselves, yet, but at least we have their example in front of us, to learn from and copy. (Someone might like to try copying one of the skills.)

When Jesus came, it was like being able to see God's way of living – in person. 'So that's what it means to love God and love one another!' people thought. 'So that's what God's love for us is like!' And even though we may not yet be able to do it very well, at least we have a wonderful example to learn from and copy.

If we're still full of bitterness about something that happened to us long ago, we can look at Jesus and copy his forgiving. If we're looking down on someone because they aren't as clever or rich as us, we can look at Jesus and copy his way of enjoying people and accepting them for what they are. If we are always worrying about clothes and possessions, we can look at Jesus and copy his simple way of living, and spend our energy cultivating the treasures that we can take with us to heaven. So Jesus is like a living 'Way' – he's a walking, talking Way to live.

In fact that's what Jesus called himself in John 14:6; he said, 'I am the Way, the Truth and the Life'. With Jesus we go one better than having his example to copy – since the Resurrection we can have his life living in us! That would be rather like our experts being able to fill us with all that makes them able to do those clever things. Imagine what a skilled church we would be if that were possible! We'd all be expert ironers, football dribblers, jugglers and cartwheelers! Well, I have to tell you that we can't do that. As humans we have to pass on our skills the hard way, by teaching and learning. But with Jesus it's different. He really can live in our lives, enabling us to love God and one another. All we need to do is invite him into our personal lives and our church, and be prepared to be gradually transformed.

Life and death

Make a circle of chairs near where you are talking, or a circle of rope – something which is clearly visible.

Explain that this circle is like our life here on earth. How do we get into it? By being born. (Invite a couple of people to make their way in.) While we're here what do we do? We eat, play, work, talk, make friends (and perhaps some enemies), watch TV, learn things and so on. (Everyone can add to the list.) Invite the people in the circle of life to mime some of those things as they are suggested.

How do we get out of the circle of life? By being born backwards? We get out of this life by dying. (The volunteers make their way out of the circle.) Point out that they're not in the circle any more, but they're in a huge space, much bigger than they might have imagined, if they'd only ever known life in the circle. And outside this space is the whole outdoors, stretching outwards and upwards, and full of light and colour, better than anything we could imagine if we'd only ever known the circle as 'life'. Just as the circle isn't the only place, so this earthly life isn't all there is to complete life – Jesus told us that life after our death can be full, rich and wonderful; and it's Jesus who has made that possible for us.

Remind everyone of the story in Mark 5:21-24, 35-43, about a twelve-year-old girl dying. Everyone is specially sad when a young person dies, because they haven't had a chance to live very long here and enjoy our world. But Jesus brings that young girl back to life again. It's as if from inside the circle of life he calls to her on the outside and she comes back in again, completely better, and hungry. He could do that because Jesus *is* life. When she next died, perhaps after a long and happy time on earth, she closed her eyes on earthly life and heard Jesus calling her name again into life – but this time from heaven, into the life with Jesus that lasts for ever.

When we get to the point of our death, Jesus will be there, calling us out into that life, and welcoming us. And because we know his voice, from a lifetime of prayer, we'll be very happy to move towards it and find him, waiting for us there.

Jesus prepares for suffering

Bring with you a box of assorted sweets or chocolates, and invite a couple of volunteers to choose one. Ask them why they chose it (there may be no reason at all) and whether they are happy with the choice they made.

All our life long we are faced with making choices. Sometimes the choice isn't that important; if you make a mistake and choose a chocolate which isn't a favourite, you haven't lost out much. But sometimes the choices are more important. Invite a couple of car owners to talk about their choice of car and whether they are happy with their decision. Ask a student which A levels they have chosen to take, or which degree course, and a child what they have chosen to do for a birthday treat.

Sometimes we have to choose even more important things than that! Let's look at a very hard choice Jesus had to make, in John 12:20-33. Jesus knew that he was alive on earth for a very important mission – he was here to save the world, and he really wanted to do that, because he loved the people. But there was a problem. He also knew that saving the world was bound to land him in terrible pain and danger, more pain and agony than anyone has ever faced before or since. It would involve taking on himself all the sin and evil of the world, and going on loving right through it.

So he had the choice – to go ahead with saving the world, taking on the suffering as part of the deal, or to avoid all that appalling suffering by opting out, in which case the world would have no hope of being saved.

And it wasn't an easy thing to choose. Everything human in him screamed out against going through the pain of it all; but everything divine in him pleaded for love and compassion, and selfless giving whatever the cost.

We know what Jesus chose. Love won, and he chose to go through hell, giving up everything, including his life, just so that we could be set free to live.

Jesus suffered for us

Ask two people to come out and stand at least three metres apart. Ask one of the people to walk down to reach the other. Was there any problem in that? (Hopefully not.) Now ask both people to get to you, only this time with one condition – they mustn't move. Can they do it? (No, it's impossible.) If they want to get across to reach you they will have to go on a journey to do it. Is the journey easy or difficult? (They can try it to find out.) They probably did that with no trouble at all.

But suppose the journey is made very difficult? (Tie all four ankles together with a scarf and walk away from them.) Can they get to me now? (Let them try.) As they are moving along explain that they can certainly do it, but only by using a lot more effort, and with quite a struggle. Stop them halfway and explain how being crucified was like a terrible journey that Jesus had to make to rescue us. In the middle of his journey people shouted at him to come down from the cross and save himself from the suffering.

Ask the people if they would be capable of untying the scarf and walking free. So could Jesus have come down from the cross, so why didn't he? He did it because there wasn't any other way to rescue us apart from accepting all the chains of our sin and carrying them for us, even though it made his journey so difficult. So instead of opting out, he carried on (the people can carry on too) until the journey was finished so we can all be set free (untie the legs of the volunteers).

The Servant King

Bring along a crown and robe, some pretend bags of money, a dish of fruit and two fans on sticks as shown below. Drape some cloth over a chair.

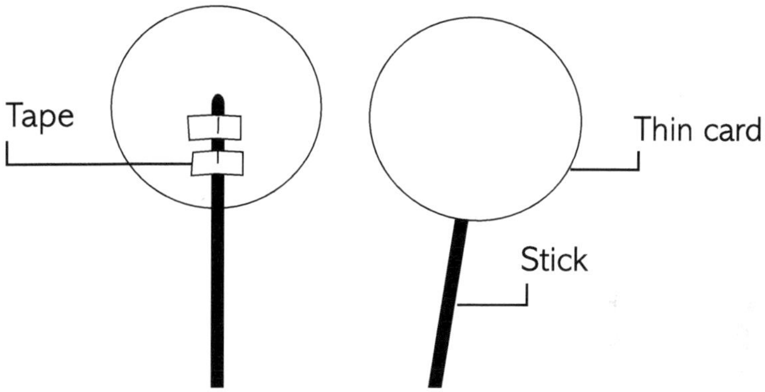

Tell everyone that today we are celebrating that Jesus Christ is King for ever. Ask a volunteer to come out and dress them up in the grand robe of very costly material, hand-embroidered by expert craftsmen, and the solid gold crown, studded with real diamonds and rubies. Sit the king on a grand throne covered in pure silk and made from finest marble, and provide him with some servants to stand around and wave him with fans, bowing before him. Give him bags of money on a table nearby, and provide a dish of fresh fruits for him to snack on between banquets.

Is this right? Is this what King Jesus is really like? No, it's all wrong! Although Jesus has been given all power and majesty and honour, and is King of all time and space, he is a very different sort of king. He lays aside his majesty (help the king up from his throne), lays aside his robe and his crown (take them from him), lays aside all wealth and comfort (the servants move the table), so that he can be one with us (he shakes hands with the servants) and live among us, caring for us, searching for the lost, and binding up the injured. (Thank the servants and the king for their help.)

Now if that's how our king behaves, then that's how we are to behave as well. If we worship and honour a Servant King, who doesn't greedily look after his own needs all the time but makes a point of looking after other people's needs, then that's what we have to do! Our wealth and treasure will be in loving service, wherever we're needed. That's how Jesus will recognise us as his people, when we get to the gate of heaven.

Putting things together

Bring in some kind of game or piece of equipment which needs putting together and setting up properly before it can be used. This could be anything from a computer to a folding bed – it all depends on what is available and the interest area of the congregation. It needs to have a set of instructions to go with it.

Begin by introducing your item of equipment. Pretend that you are having a real problem with this thing because you don't understand it at all. You don't understand how to get it to work.

Have a primed helper who comes up at this stage and shows you the instruction leaflet. They tell you that if you read that it will tell you how the thing works and how to use it. Be surprised, but set to reading some of the instructions, without relating them to the equipment. They don't make much sense to you, and you get fed up. It's no good – you don't understand and it doesn't make sense.

Explain that this is rather like the way the two disciples felt as they walked sadly back home on the very first Easter Day (see Luke 24:13-35). They didn't understand anything any more. They had great hopes about Jesus, but now he was dead, so their hopes were dead as well. They had heard about the women saying they had seen Jesus alive early that morning, but that didn't make any sense to them either. How on earth could someone be dead as dead and now be alive? It couldn't possibly be true!

Just then someone joined them and asked what they were so sad about. And when they told him, he started to show them how it actually did make a lot of sense. (Break off as the helper comes and offers to take you through the instructions and sort the equipment out. Accept their help and marvel as gradually, step by step, it starts to come together, and eventually works. Be excited about this and thank the helper. Then come back to the Emmaus story.)

Well, it certainly helps to have someone who really understands to help you when you are in a muddle! That's how those disciples felt when the stranger explained that it was all there in the scriptures (pick up a Bible) about the promised Messiah having to suffer and die before there could be new life. When they reached their home they invited the helpful stranger in to stay with them, and when their guest took the bread and blessed and broke it (mime this) . . . what do you think they suddenly realised?

It was Jesus!

And that is still what Jesus does. He walks along with us where we are walking. He helps us understand about God through the words of scripture (pick up the Bible again), he helps us make sense of life and its problems (stand beside the working piece of equipment), and he makes himself known to us in the breaking of bread.

Jesus can save us

First ask everyone to imagine that someone has just staggered into church and they've been shot. (You could have a pre-warned accomplice to act this out.) Assure everyone that this is only pretend, but if it happened, what could we do? He might be begging us to help him and get the bullet out (he begs for help) but we know that if Mrs Eastoe or Mark or David Stowe tried to put things right our poor injured person would probably die (loud moans and more begging for help). Can anyone think of someone who would be able to help him? It would have to be a surgeon at the hospital. So we would get the ambulance, and they would get him into the operating theatre. Now if the surgeon can't be bothered because he's having his lunch and reading the newspaper, our friend will definitely die (feeble moans). But it's much more likely that the surgeon cuts him open very carefully, sews up the bits that need sewing up, and soon our friend is fine again and can go home. (The patient thanks everyone, enthusing over what the surgeon has done for him, and walks out of church waving cheerfully.)

We are all damaged and injured by our selfishness, our guilt, our vanity, bad temper and so on. The only person who can save our lives and set us free to live in harmony with God is someone who is both God and human. Is there anyone who fits that description? Jesus does. Will he want to bother with us lot, though? Yes, he certainly does. Because he loves us, he came to live among us and he died for us. After he came to life again he went back to heaven, and we are joining with all the angels and saints in heaven today in saying, 'Thank you, Jesus – we think what you did was wonderful, and we think you're brilliant, and we love you' (or words to that effect).

A hero's welcome

Beforehand ask a few people to bring awards they have been given. These should include things that probably lots of others have as well, such as a five-metre swimming badge and a driving licence. There may also be a darts cup or a music certificate.

Begin by showing the awards and talking briefly to the award-holders about how these have been well earned, and give us an idea of the standard that has been achieved, so they are something to celebrate. Probably lots of us have similar awards that we have been honoured with, which is well worth celebrating. (A round of applause may be in order.)

When Jesus entered heaven, about forty days after he had come back to life on the first Easter Day, the whole of heaven gave him a hero's welcome. They said he was worthy to receive power and wealth and wisdom and strength, honour and glory and praise – everything good they could think of (see Revelation 5:12).

They wanted to honour him like this because Jesus had managed to do such an incredible thing. He had lived a human life and gone on loving all the way through it without once giving in to temptation, turning against God's will or putting his own wants first. Through loving people enough to die for them, he had been able to break the hold death has over all of us, so we can live freely and happily in God's company. (Another huge round of applause for Jesus.)

Now go back to the swimming badge. This badge proves that Susie is able to swim. What God is saying to us today is that Jesus has won the victory for us, so we are all able to live this incredible new, free and happy life in his company.

It is as if there's a wonderful pool just waiting for us to enjoy, but perhaps we're only holding our badges at the edge of the pool, instead of getting into the water and using them. Let's plunge into the life Jesus has won for us and enjoy it to the full!

Jesus sets us free

You will need some lengths of rope, chain or thick string, a blindfold and a bicycle lock with padlock.

Talk about how we often tie our lives up in knots. They may remember having done something wrong and then having told a few lies to cover up. Or there may be some who have once had a row with someone and now dread bumping into that person ever again. Those kinds of experiences are rather like pieces of rope tying us up and preventing us from moving freely. (Ask for a volunteer who will help by allowing you to tie them up here and there.)

There are other things which chain us as well. Pick out a really strong rope or chain and explain how selfishness ties us up and restricts our movement dreadfully – we're so busy thinking about ourselves, our own needs and wants, our own rights and so on that we can't reach out to other people at all. (Tie up the arms firmly.)

Arrogance and vanity make us think we're so wonderful that they stop us seeing the truth about ourselves (put on the blindfold) and fear and guilt can make us too terrified to move forward (tie up the legs).

So we end up spiritually trussed up, living a compromise and never living life as fully as we could.

Jesus loves us and hates seeing us like this; he yearns to set us free, and the good news is that he can. When we hesitantly let him into our lives he will start untying our ropes of selfishness, taking off our blindfolds of arrogance and vanity, unchaining our fear and guilt (do this with the ropes, etc.) until he has set us free to live happily and love others. (The volunteer can caper around a bit to demonstrate.)

The Holy Spirit

The fire of the Spirit

Beforehand make five red, yellow and orange flame shapes (about 30 centimetres high) and hide them around the church.

Begin by asking for examples of flames, such as on a gas hob, bonfire, forest fire, log fire, candle, acetylene torch, fire-eater, house on fire, match, oil lamp, steel works, steam engine, lighter, Bunsen burner. Draw people's attention to the tremendous power of some of these and the quiet, gentle nature and soft light of others. Fire is something we all have to respect, as it can burn and destroy as well as giving us light and heat.

Send the children off to search for the five flames that are hidden in the church, and tell the adults about our need to seek out the Spirit expecting to find, just as the children are doing now. They trust that what they have been told to search for will be there, and it will. We need to believe that if we seek God we will find him – and we will.

When the children return with the five flames, you can remind everyone of the way the Holy Spirit is described in Acts 2:2, 3 as being like tongues of fire, with the sound of a rushing wind. (You can get everyone to make this sound as the flame-carriers run round the church.)

Like fire, the Spirit can be strong and powerful in our lives. (The first flame is held up.) Sometimes the Spirit is gentle and quiet, whispering deep into our needs and telling us what is right. (The second flame is held up.) Like fire, the Spirit is warming, spreading love and a real desire to put things right, and stand up for goodness and truth. (The third flame is held up.) Like fire the Spirit is purifying, burning away all that is evil and selfish in us, so that we can become like pure refined gold, glowing with the light of God's love. (The fourth flame is held up.) And, like fire, the Spirit is enlightening, shedding light for us on the Bible, our conversations and relationships and the events of our lives, so that we can see God more clearly through them. (The fifth flame is held up.)

The wind of the Spirit

You will need a hand-held hairdryer (and possibly an extension lead).

Begin by talking about the wind, and how we can tell it is windy, even though the wind itself is invisible. Collect examples of the signs from the congregation. Draw together the signs with the principle that wind makes things move.

Now ask some volunteers to scatter some cut-out paper people on the ground, fixing some firmly to the ground with Blu-tack or paperweights. In John 3:1-8 we overhear a conversation between Jesus and a man called Nicodemus. We know Nicodemus was a Pharisee, and knew lots of clever things. But Jesus puzzled him. He could see that the miracles Jesus was doing made it look as if Jesus really was God's promised Messiah who they were all waiting for. The problem was, Jesus didn't seem to be sticking rigidly to the rules Nicodemus and the other Pharisees felt he ought to be. He seemed far too broad-minded. He was spending time with sinners.

The good thing about Nicodemus was that he didn't keep his worries to himself, or pretend they weren't there, or reject Jesus because he was making him think about things in a new way. He went to find Jesus one night and talked to him about it all. And that's what we need to do with all our doubts and puzzles and questions.

Jesus gave him some funny answers, and one of the answers was about the wind. He said that living in the Spirit is rather like being blown by the wind. God wants to move us along and he can do that so long as we don't fix ourselves down. Watch how the wind from the hairdryer can move these people. (Switch on the hairdryer and blow the people along.)

Look at these people who were stuck down to the floor. The wind blew but they haven't moved anywhere. And sometimes we are like that. We might sing on Sundays about wanting to live in God's Spirit, but when that means being ready to move or change in our life or our attitudes or ideas, we start fixing ourselves to the floor where we feel safer, and can enjoy moving a little to the breath of God, but not enough to be actually moved along.

So let's work at being brave enough to come to Jesus with the deep worries and puzzles of life, knowing that God is quite able to cope with them and won't suddenly disappear or be offended. And let's work at being brave enough to stand out in the wind of God's Spirit, without fixing ourselves to the spot, but willing for him to move us as a church and as individuals wherever he wants to move us.

God in our boots

Bring along a pair of wellington boots which fit you, or arrange beforehand for a volunteer to bring their boots and do the actions as you talk.

Stand the boots together where they can be seen, and explain that these boots (being very keen, conscientious boots) want to walk wherever you go. (Walk about and watch the boots, still sitting there and not moving.) They are trying very hard, but they don't seem to be getting anywhere, do they? Perhaps they need a bit of encouragement. (Some of the children can encourage the boots from a distance!)

Poor old boots – they'd love to be walking where you walk, but they just can't manage it. Why not? Because they haven't got you inside them!

Climb into the boots and see the difference. Suddenly they are able to walk around wherever you walk. They can even jump with you, run with you and dance with you! And all because they have you in them.

In the first chapter of Genesis nothing happened, nothing was drawn into life, until God's Spirit made creation happen. And in Acts chapter 2 the disciples weren't changed until they'd received the Holy Spirit. We can know lots about Jesus and what he did on earth and what he said, and that can make us very keen to live like him – in a loving, generous, honest way. But unless we ask God to be in us, getting to know him as a person, rather than a set of facts, or a bit of a history lesson, we'll be like the boots on their own, wanting to move with God, but not able to do it on their own. (As you say this, take off the boots and put them on their own while you move around.)

As soon as we ask God into our life, his Spirit comes and moves in us (put the boots on again), and that makes it possible for us to go wherever God wants us to go, and act as God wants us to act. The Spirit of God which was seen settling on Jesus when John baptised him in the river Jordan, settles on all of God's children as they put their faith and trust in him.

So let's not waste our time trying hard to do good things *for* God like a pair of boots without any living feet in them. Instead, let's invite the Spirit of God every day to come and fill us, so God's life is *in* us, and can let us dance through life with praise, walk beside those who need our help, and stick to the right path all the way to heaven.

Spirit-filled saints

Bring with you something to inflate, such as a beach ball, or a travel neck-cushion, or a balloon.

Begin by playing a snippet of *When the saints go marching in,* reminding everyone of all the saints who have gone marching into heaven, and we also want to be among that number one day.

But what is a saint? You may have some windows with particular saints on. If so, you can briefly draw people's attention to these, and any saintly connections your church or town has. Emphasise that although these may be importantly fixed in stained glass now, in their lives they were ordinary people. We may well have lots of saints sitting here now, because we are all called to be saints, or God's holy people.

How can you spot a holy person when you meet one? The way they think and talk and behave makes you realise that they are full of God's loving Spirit. Show your inflatable. It was designed to be full of air, so at the moment, without air in it, it isn't really able to be properly itself. Ask someone to breathe into it to inflate it. Can we see the air that has been breathed in? No. Can we see the difference it makes? Yes! It has turned this ball/cushion/balloon into what it was designed to be, so now it is really itself, and also very useful.

We can't see the loving Spirit of God either. But whenever people are filled with it, they are able to be more fully their true selves, and it shows in their love for God and their love for others. Lots of inflatables have a valve which stops the air coming in until it is deliberately opened. With us, too, there has to be a definite decision to open up to God's in-breathing of his Spirit. What the saints have done and are doing is keeping that valve open, so that they can be filled with the Spirit, and topped up whenever they get a bit deflated.

One saint – Paul – wrote about the whole church being filled with the Holy Spirit of God. The Church isn't supposed to have loads of deflated Christians and one or two saints here and there who are full of God's loving Spirit. The idea of the church is that *everyone* in it is full of the breath of God!

Let God fill you up with his life, and make you into the person he knows you can be. We'll all look different shapes, and we'll all be useful to the world in different ways, just as a beachball is useful for throwing around but not so good as a pillow or a camping mattress. But as God breathes his loving Spirit into us more and more, we will become more and more our true selves – holy people the world needs, marching into God's kingdom with all the other saints.

Guided by the Spirit

First fill the space of the centre aisle with chairs and obstacles. If yours is a fixed pews building, have people to sit down as obstacles in the aisle. Remind everyone of how Jesus was talking to his friends at the last supper they had together before he was crucified. Jesus knew his friends were dreading the future without him being there with them. Perhaps they thought it would be a bit like this.

Ask for a volunteer and blindfold them, twizzle them round and send them off down the aisle. As they walk hesitantly, bumping into the obstacles, you talk about Jesus' friends thinking that living without Jesus around would be like trying to get round the difficulties of life blindfolded, and with no one to help or guide them.

Rescue the volunteer and remove their blindfold. As this person knows, you don't feel very safe all on your own and unable to see where the obstacles are. It is frightening and could be dangerous. Sometimes our life can feel like that, and it isn't a comfortable place to be.

What Jesus wants his friends to know is that God doesn't have that in mind for them at all. Although Jesus knew he wouldn't be there physically with his friends for ever, he promised them that they (and we) would have a personal guide right there with us. Let's see how that changes things for us.

Blindfold the volunteer again, but this time appoint a sensible, caring guide who steers them round the obstacles, talking to them and helping them along. (You may want to have primed this person beforehand.)

Watch them together, and then talk alongside the rest of their journey about God's Holy Spirit being with us to teach and explain things to us, to guide us and help us through the dangerous parts of life, so that we are not left alone, but working in partnership with our loving God.

Christian discipleship

Total commitment

You will need someone who can do gymnastics or dance. Ask them to prepare a sequence of moves which need total commitment in order to work, such as somersaults and cartwheels, pirouettes and arabesques.

Begin by asking the gymnasts or dancers to perform their demonstration. Briefly interview them, thanking them and asking whether they could do these things first time, or whether they had to practise. Draw attention to the commitment that has to be given to anything you want to do really well. You can't 'half do' some of those moves, or you'd probably fall flat on your face.

As Christians we are called to that same kind of commitment. We can't 'half do' it. When we commit ourselves to following Christ, it's going to affect the way we talk, the way we behave with our friends and our enemies, the way we spend our time and our money. It's going to affect all our thinking and the choices we make. So it's a bit like deciding to do a double somersault, or a triple pirouette – it takes a lot of dedication and courage to launch off.

Imagine if you were just launching yourself into a triple somersault and all your strength suddenly wasn't there. You'd certainly notice it was missing! In fact, you wouldn't be able to do any of those clever moves without strength.

In our Christian life, God's Holy Spirit is the strength. He enables us to do those triple somersaults of caring love for those we don't much like, and the double pirouettes of co-operating when all we want is our own way. Real loving is very hard work, and it takes lots of dedication. With God's strength we can do it, and then we will be moving freely and beautifully through life, in the way God called us to, and knows will make us, and others, truly happy.

Obedience

Begin by asking for some volunteers to read the following conversations.

1. **Mum:** David, it's time to stop playing and go to bed now.
   David: Oh, but Mum, I'm much too busy!
2. **Dad:** Turn that music down, Gary!!
   Gary: But I like it, and it needs to be loud!!
3. **Hilda:** George, it's time you gave up smoking.
   George: But, Hilda, it's my decision, and none of your business.
4. **Fred:** Now, Mother, you need to wear a hearing aid.
   Mother: What's that, Fred?
   Fred: A HEARING AID! YOU NEED TO WEAR ONE, MOTHER.
   Mother: No, I don't – I can hear perfectly when people bother to speak up properly!

All through our lives we're supposed to be obedient, and all through our lives we prefer to do as we like!

Today we're going to look at what it means to be obedient, and why it's a good thing to work at, even though we all find it so very difficult to do what we're told.

Scatter the ten commandments, written on pieces of card, over the aisle, or stick them with Blu-tack on to pillars.

In Exodus 20:1-17 we can read the ten commandments – ten useful rules to help us live God's way. These rules were given to the people through Moses, the great leader who had led the people out of slavery in Egypt. They've all been in the desert for quite a long time, learning to be God's people. And then God gives them the Law, which they are told to obey. They are still good rules, and when Jesus came he didn't say, 'Listen, everyone, now I've come you don't need to bother with all those commandments any more!' Jesus insisted that he had come not to destroy the Law but to fulfil it, to fill it full of God's love.

So Jesus summed all the rules up in two parcels. Produce one bag labelled 'Love God' and another one labelled 'Love one another', and sort out the first four commandments into the first bag and the second six into the second bag. That makes them easier for us to carry around in our heads (hold a bag in each hand), but we need to remember what's inside each bag, and take them out to look at from time to time, like we've done today.

So Jesus thought it was good to be obedient. He was obedient to his heavenly Father, even when that turned out to mean he had to die on the cross! The reason he was obedient was because he really understood why it was important.

If we understand the reason for being obedient, we're much more likely to try and do what we're told. If Fred's mother really understood how difficult it was becoming for the family to talk to her without her hearing aid, she'd *want* to wear it. If Gary really understood how hard it was for his Dad to concentrate on his work with the music so loud, he'd *want* to turn it down a bit.

In other words, obedience is all to do with acting out of love. As we get to understand and love God better, we shall find we are more and more keen to do what he wants us to.

Baptism

Using a flipchart or large sheet of paper and thick pens, collect everyone's suggestions about what water can do. Some of the suggestions can be drawn rather than written, so that the non-readers can also join in.

Read through all the suggestions to celebrate them, and talk about how Baptism picks up on these qualities of water and uses them to teach us spiritual things. When we are baptised we are 'drowned' to the old ways, given new life, washed clean, and refreshed. If it is practical, have water in the font and pour it as you explain each quality and its spiritual meaning.

Remind everyone about Jesus being baptised, and how, as he was praying, the Holy Spirit came upon him, looking rather like a dove flying down to rest on him. And God told Jesus that he was God's Son, and God was well pleased with him (see Matthew 3:13-17).

Point out any dove symbols there are in the church – in carvings, pictures or windows – and have a cut-out dove shape (you can use the picture below) to show everyone. The dove has become a sign or symbol for the Holy Spirit because of what happened at the Baptism of Jesus.

When we are baptised God calls us actually by name to follow him, and sets us apart to love and serve him through the whole of our life. We can only do that with the gift of the Holy Spirit, so that is what we are given. The more we use it, the more it will grow. The sign of the dove will remind us. Whenever we see a dove or a pigeon, or a wild goose, it will remind us that we belong to God, and have chosen to follow him.

Seeing ourselves

You will need a mirror. First do a spot of face-painting on a volunteer, writing their own name in mirror-writing across their face. Then show them their face in the mirror. They will be surprised at what they look like because it isn't their familiar face looking back at them. Yet it is their own named self they are looking at.

Whenever Jesus met up with people he seems to have been able to show them who they were; what they were really like. By the things he said, the stories he told, and by the signs and miracles he did, people were able to look at him and suddenly see something about themselves they hadn't realised before. Some suddenly realised that they were lovable and important, when they had always thought they were rubbish. Others suddenly saw that they were living very mean, selfish lives, and knew they wanted to change.

In the story told in Luke 5:1-11, Simon Peter has been fishing all night long without any success at all. It's possible that Jesus had watched them, and noticed how they carried on even when they were tired and disappointed. Perhaps Jesus brought that into his teaching, and the fishermen would have sat up on the beach and thought, 'This man really knows what it's like to be a fisherman like me, working all night with nothing to show for it!' So when Jesus suggested they try again, Simon was doubtful, but willing to give it a go. The huge catch of fish, coming suddenly after all that time they had worked in vain, must have given Simon a shock. It was a bit like looking in a mirror and seeing who he really was for the first time.

He saw that this man Jesus, who had been sitting in Simon's own fishing boat talking to the crowds, was different from anyone he had ever met before. His goodness, his wise teaching and his knowledge of where the fish were, all made Simon suddenly ashamed. We don't know what it was in Simon's life that went through his mind. It might have been some particular sin he still felt guilty about, or it might have been remembering all the general meanness and selfishness, or the bad temper he knew he had.

The important thing for us to look at is how Jesus helped him see himself, and then said, 'Don't be afraid, follow me.' That is what Jesus does with us today as well. So be ready for it. If something makes you suddenly see yourself and you don't like everything you see, Jesus will not be standing at your elbow, saying, 'There's no hope for you, then, is there? You might as well give up.' He will be there, speaking into your heart words of love and comfort and hope: 'Don't be afraid of what you really are. Come and follow me.'

Ready for the race?

Beforehand prepare a number of heavy carrier bags and a rucksack, and have a sack or strong dustbin bag. Label the bags 'I want my own way', 'It isn't fair', 'So what?', 'I'll never forgive them' and 'No one will notice'. Also bring the local school's PE kit.

Begin by showing everyone the PE kit and draw from them what it is, who wears it, and why we do PE dressed like this instead of in our best clothes, or in bridesmaids' dresses, or Mickey Mouse suits. Establish that it's more practical and comfortable to wear light clothes like this which don't get in the way of our running and jumping.

Refer to the letter to the Hebrew Christians (see Hebrews 12:1, 2) in which following Jesus through our lives is said to be a bit like running a race: we need to look where we're going. That means keeping our eyes on Jesus and his way of living. This will keep us on the right track in our own lives, reminding us to be honest instead of telling lies, thinking of other people's needs instead of just wanting our own way, and sharing our ideas and fears with God instead of ignoring him most of the time.

But often we run our Christian life in very unsuitable clothes. At this point ask for a volunteer, and load them up with all the bags, explaining what each represents, and how we weigh ourselves down with all this luggage. As you hand over the sack for them to stand in, point out how difficult we make it for ourselves by hanging on to all these attitudes which make Christian living extra hard. The volunteer can try running to prove the point.

Today we are being given a useful tip for Christian living: get rid of all these unhelpful habits (name them as you take them from the volunteer), so that we are free to run God's race-track uncluttered and 'light'. Then we can concentrate on Jesus, and learn to live his way – the way of love.

Spreading the good news

Bring with you a newspaper, a TV remote control, a mobile phone, an airmail letter and, if possible, a trumpeter (failing a real one, a recorded version will do nicely).

Begin by picking up the newspaper and reading out a few headlines. Talk about this being one of the ways we use to get other people to hear our news. People used to use a town crier. (You could ask a loud-voiced volunteer to demonstrate. The news they bellow is written on a piece of paper: 'There is only one real God. He made us and he loves us!') Pick up the remote control and explain that now we don't have to shout so loud because we invite the town criers into our homes and sit them in the corner to tell us the latest news. We can even switch them off!

Another thing people used was a trumpeter. (Have this demonstrated briefly.) That got people's attention so they would listen to what you were saying. Now we have this to get people's attention, and get them listening to us. (Demonstrate the mobile phone.) People used to send their news by pigeons, and now we send it on a metal bird. (Show the airmail letter.)

What has stayed the same all through the years is that people always want to pass on their news. And in Romans 10:9-15 we are told that the news the town crier shouted to us (they can do it again) is such good news, not just for us but for everyone, that we need to make sure we pass it on. Like honey or peanut butter, we are not to keep the good news to ourselves, but spread it!

We can tell people about God's love by behaving in a kind and loving way, by being generous with our time and money, by praying for our friends and for difficult situations, by living by God's rules, and by bringing our faith into the conversation instead of only mentioning it among our church friends. And who knows, God may also call some of you to tell the good news as newspaper reporters, in government, on television or as a famous sports star. However you do it, do it!

Prayer and Bible study

Bring along (or ask someone else in the congregation to bring) something which you have made or are making, which requires lots of persistence and perseverance (such as a garment or model, diary or recipe). Talk about the struggle you have had keeping going with it. Use parts of the church building, particularly if it is an ancient one, and draw everyone's attention to some piece of stained glass or carving, and all the persistence and hard work that went into making it. Emphasise the value of doing these things, even though they are difficult.

Jesus tells us to keep going with our prayer, and never give up. Suggest a pattern of praying when you wake up, before you eat a meal, and before you go to sleep at night, showing large posters of logos for these (as below). Or they can be shown on a screen. If we get into a prayer habit like this, we will be deepening our friendship with God, and getting to know him better.

There is another good habit we need to have as well as praying, and that is reading the Bible every day. There are lots of books and schemes to help us, and we can choose one which suits our age, interests and experience. If we don't know much about the Bible there are people in the church to talk it over with.

However we read it, it's important to pray and read God's word in Scripture so that we really can have God's law of love remembered in our minds and written on our hearts. That way we will be ready for any jobs God asks us to do, and we will be better able to hear him speaking into our lives.

The way of the cross

You will need two lengths of bramble, and gardening gloves to handle them. If you can get hold of a length of chain as well, this would be excellent; otherwise, rope, or a paper chain will do fine.

Lay the two lengths of bramble to form a cross on the floor, explaining what you are doing for the benefit of those who will not be able to see this. Make the point that you are wearing protective gloves as the brambles are painful. Explain that the brambles represent all the suffering and pain of the cross. Ask for a volunteer to stand at the top end of the cross. This person represents all of us humans, chained up in all the sin and selfishness that stops us from living freely. (Chain their hands together.) Ask another volunteer to stand at the foot end of the cross, some distance from it. This person represents Jesus.

In Matthew 16:16 we hear how Simon Peter was ready to speak out the truth he had realised about Jesus – that Jesus was the Christ, the Son of the living God. Jesus knew his friends had to be sure of this before they could cope with the next stage of the plan. Now that was in place, and it was time for Jesus to get his friends ready for what had to happen next (see Matthew16:21-25).

Jesus couldn't just go on working in one part of our world, because he had come into the world to save all of us. That would mean walking a very painful road – the way of the cross. The pain of giving his life on the cross was the only way for Jesus to be able to reach us and set us free. He couldn't get round it; he had to go through with it, even though he knew it would hurt.

Ask the person who is representing Jesus to take their shoes off and start walking towards the cross. Before they get there, stop them as you remind people how Simon Peter couldn't bear to think of his friend going through all that pain, and said, 'Never, Lord! This shall not happen to you!' But if Jesus had listened to him (walk round to the representative human in chains), we would never have been set free from the sin that imprisons us. Never. There would have been no hope for us any more.

(Go back to 'Jesus'.) The good and wonderful news is that Jesus loved us far too much to let his own suffering stop him from saving us. Today we won't make Lawrence walk barefoot over those brambles, but as we think of Jesus gladly stepping out to Jerusalem, where he knew he would meet terrible pain and suffering, let's thank him in our hearts for loving us so much that he was prepared to do it anyway (walk round to the human in chains) so that we could all be set free. (Set the person free.)

Mary and Martha

Beforehand make a pair of large card ears, about 30 centimetres high, and a pair of large card hands, about the same size.

Start by asking for two volunteers, one of whom holds the ears to the side of her head, and the other who has the hands fixed to her own hands with large rubber bands. Remind everyone of the two people in Luke 10:38-42, both very good friends of Jesus. Their names were Martha and Mary and they were sisters. Jesus often went round to the home where they lived with their brother Lazarus, and they all enjoyed one another's company.

Alice is like a cartoon picture of Mary, because what she liked to do was sit and listen to Jesus and she could listen to him for hours. She probably liked listening to all sorts of people, and may have been the kind of person people could talk easily to because they could see she was interested in them. Mary's idea of cooking a meal was probably beans on toast, and she probably didn't notice the dust creeping up until she could write in it.

Laura is like a cartoon picture of Martha, because what she liked best was doing things for people and making sure they had clean shirts and well-balanced meals. Her idea of cooking a meal would be something like roast chicken with all the trimmings. If you wanted something done, you'd ask Martha.

Now people sometimes get upset by this story because they think Jesus is saying that everyone ought to spend their time listening like Mary, and that busy, practical people like Martha aren't somehow as good. But, of course, Jesus isn't saying that at all. His own life was full of work and activity, travelling, preaching, teaching and healing, and none of that would have got done if he hadn't been a doer.

But he also spent hours late at night, or early in the morning on his own with God, talking things over and quietly listening. And he knew that this was a really important part of the doing. He knew we need to keep the right balance between input (the ears) and output (the hands). On that particular visit to Martha and Mary's house, the listening was more important than the doing. What we all have to do is notice when we need to listen, and be ready to stop what we're doing and listen.

All of us need to set aside a quiet time to be with God morning and night, every day. It doesn't have to be long, but it has to be there. If we neglect that, our ability to discern right behaviour will start to slip, and we risk sliding into the kind of life that hurts God so much. Spending time quietly with God is not an optional extra for people with time on their hands, it's an absolute necessity, as well as being refreshing, rejuvenating and problem solving!

Serving two masters

You will need to prepare this talk with another adult. The two of you will be bosses, standing at either end of the church.

Begin by asking for a volunteer who doesn't mind doing a few jobs. This person stands halfway down the church, and you introduce them to the two bosses they are to work for this morning. They are to serve both people as well as they can.

First one boss gives an order, such as to put three chairs out in a line in the middle of the church. As soon as this is done, the other boss gets annoyed that the chairs are arranged like this and tells the servant to put only two chairs out, facing different ways. The first boss tells the servant to put a hymn book on each chair. The other boss tells the servant to put the hymn books away and put a Bible on each chair. Continue the orders so that the poor servant is running about the church pleasing no one.

Thank the volunteer, and explain how Jesus said in Matthew 6:24 that it is impossible to serve two bosses like that. Either you end up loving the first and hating the second, or hating the first and loving the second. It is the same with trying to serve God while we are still bound up with materialism, money and possessions. (Have two signs: 'God' and 'Worldly Riches'. These can include appropriate symbols, such as a cross and some money.) It simply can't be done. While God is whispering to your conscience to live simply and generously, Worldly Riches is insisting that you get the latest fashion in clothes or music. While God is expecting you to commit time to prayer and Bible reading, Worldly Riches is expecting you to commit that time to reading the latest magazines and watching the latest videos.

If we choose to serve God (display the 'God' sign) we have to choose not to serve Worldly Riches. (Tear up the 'Worldly Riches' sign.)

Serving or being served?

Have three chairs placed in front of the altar, in the obvious place of honour. Prepare three 'Reserved' signs.

In Mark 10:35-37 we see two of Jesus' disciples – James and John – coming up to him with a question they wanted to ask. They wanted to make sure Jesus would give them what they wanted, so instead of starting with the real question, they first said, 'We want you to do for us whatever we ask.' Perhaps we try that one with parents or spouses, or the boss sometimes. Like this.

Invite a child and adult to come and read the following script:

Child: Dad, you love me, don't you?

Dad: Yes, son.

Child: You'd give me anything I wanted, wouldn't you?

Dad: Mmm . . . maybe I would.

Child: Well, can I have this really good educational computer game?

Dad: No.

Child: Oh, but Dad, you said . . .

Dad: I only said maybe!

Child: Oh well, it was worth a try.

Jesus didn't say yes either. He asked James and John what they wanted, and was pretty gobsmacked by what it was. Invite two children to read out James and John's question – have it printed out in large, clear letters for them: 'Let one of us sit at your right and the other at your left in your glory.'

What on earth was Jesus to say to that? Point out the three chairs, and have someone place a reserved sign on the main, middle one. Who was this place in glory reserved for? Jesus. Had he pushed for it or even asked for it? No! He was given it by Almighty God, his Father. It was being a servant and being willing to give up his life for us all that brought Jesus to reign in glory. If James and John were to be granted their wish (invite them to go and sit either side of the main seat), what would it show about them, and about Jesus? (Collect ideas. It might show that they were the most important of the disciples, that Jesus liked them better than the others, that pushy people get their way in God's kingdom, for instance.)

Jesus pointed out to them that those places are not his to give anyway as they have reserved signs on them. (Invite someone to move James and John off the thrones and place reserved signs on them.) No one, not even Jesus, knew who they are reserved for. It could be for someone here! What we can be sure of is that the people they're reserved for would be the very last people to ask to sit there, or count themselves more worthy than anyone else!

Jesus tells us that we are all here to bother about serving others, not to bother about being served. Even Jesus himself, the Son of the living God, came as a servant, and gave up his life for the good of others. That's the example we're to follow, not resigning ourselves to it, grudgingly, but happy to have the honour of giving up our lives to serve others in love.

Servants or friends?

Begin with this sketch, which looks at the difference between servants and friends.

The servant

The employer is talking on his mobile phone, pacing up and down, with a file open. He's sorting out some complex problem. The office cleaner comes in with feather duster and starts cleaning.

Mr King *(Into phone)* Quite . . . Quite . . . But look at these figures on page 24 . . . *(catches sight of Marg the cleaner)* Marg, get me a strong coffee. And a doughnut or something. *(Returns to phone)* Yes, these figures should have warned us . . . Well, the point is what can we do about it now?

(Marg reappears with coffee and doughnut.)

Marg Coffee, Mr King. It's strong. And a doughnut. *(Puts them on desk)*

Mr King *(Still on phone, listening and making 'mm' noises. Motions with hand for Marg not to interrupt him as he's busy.)* Sorry, Steve, say that again . . . the schedules systematically reduced what? . . . Oh, I see. Yes, of course. So what are you going to do about it?

(Marg continues dusting.)

Mr King *(Still on phone)* Marg, get me the February file – it's there on my desk. *(Talks into phone)* It seems to me we can possibly get ourselves out of this mess, Steve. I've just had an idea.

(Marg brings the February file to Mr King.)

Marg The February file, Mr King.

Mr King *(Takes it without thanking her and starts looking in it. Into phone he says)* Yes, here it is! I'm looking at these figures for the second week of February . . .

(Marg goes back to the dusting. The desk phone rings.)

Mr King Answer that, Marg.

Marg *(Picks up phone)* Hello, Mr King's office. Well, he's very busy at the moment, in an important meeting . . . Oh, I've no idea, I'm only the cleaner here. I just do what I'm told.

The friends

Norman and Pete walk up to a bench and sit down. They put their rucksacks down.

Pete Phew! That was quite a climb, wasn't it. What a view, though, eh?

Norman Marvellous, isn't it. *(Pause)* Anyway, you were saying about your interview . . .

Pete Oh yeah, that's right. So we've got to decide whether to move or not, basically. And that's a big decision to make.

Norman How does Sheila feel about moving? She's settled here, isn't she?

Pete Yes, it would be quite a wrench for her, but you know Sheila, she's willing to give it a go if she feels it's what God wants for us.

Norman Funny, isn't it. This time last year, you were just made redundant, and no hopes for the future, and now this new door seems to be opening for you. I'm really happy for you, Pete.

Pete Thanks, Norman. Well, you've been a good friend through all this – it's always good to talk things over with you. Shall we be on our way then? *(They get up and walk off.)*

All four characters I no longer call you servants, because a servant doesn't know his master's business. Instead I have called you friends.

Invite everyone to spot the differences. Also ask those involved in the sketch what differences they felt. The kind of things which might come up are the sense of involvement and belonging which friendship gives, compared with the distance and lack of co-operation in servants; the difference in how they feel valued, and what response is acceptable.

Point out that Jesus said he was no longer thinking of us as servants but as friends. That means we are people he is happy to talk things over with, co-operate with and involve in the work. There is going to be companionship and perhaps some good-natured teasing. Above all is the sense that we are in this together, and enjoying one another's company.

Another thing Jesus said is that we are to love one another in the way he loves us. So how is that? How does Jesus love us? Collect people's ideas; here are some that occurred to me:

- as friends
- with affection
- treating us seriously
- understanding us
- with honesty
- with forgiveness
- ready to put himself out for us
- with faithfulness
- consistently

Is this how we are treating other people? Or is it how we treat the people we like? As Christians we don't have the option to choose certain people to treat with God's love, while behaving how we feel with all the rest. We can't claim to love God and then decide that some people aren't worth treating with respect or understanding.

Of course it isn't easy to love one another like this. Lots of people are difficult to love in God's way – perhaps we are, ourselves! But when we look at how amazingly God treats us, copying his way of loving is the very least we can do. And the often surprising thing is that putting ourselves out and making the effort to live God's way is very rewarding, and makes us feel much happier inside.

Follow that sign

Beforehand make a number of signs that are familiar to everyone. For example:

Show each sign in turn, and ask people: Where might you be if you saw this? How would it affect your behaviour? Now show this sign . . .

. . . and have someone carrying it round the building. Who followed this? Where did it lead to? Have the star carried round to where the crib is, with everyone following, or a representative group. From the crib show the last sign:

Remind people of how this affected John the Baptist's whole ministry, and let the sign lead people round to the font. This is the place where God leads us to commit our lives to him, ready to follow Christ and allow him to take charge. You can now use the Baptismal affirmation of faith.

The narrow gate

Beforehand prepare a narrow gateway. This may be a very narrow space between two pieces of card secured to chairs, two broom handles held close together by volunteers, or any other ingenious but simple method you think of. You will also need some big, bulky parcels, such as rolled sleeping bags, huge balloons, large cartons tied with string, etc.

First remind everyone of the narrow gate mentioned in Matthew 7:13, 14 or Luke 13:23, 24 and introduce your home-produced model. Ask for a volunteer to help explain Jesus' teaching about how to get through narrow gates. Load the volunteer up with all the bundles and parcels, either mentioning what they are or actually sticking labels on them as people suggest the things we often carry through life with us (such as resentment, I've-got-to-be-better-than-anyone-else, a cool image, I-want-it-so-I'll-have-it, me-first, and so on.)

Now let the person demonstrate what happens when s/he gets to the narrow gate. Ask them to try doing the things you suggest: first we might try to push through with everything and then get stuck; or we might try going in sideways, but that doesn't work either; or we may even squeeze through on our own and try pulling the luggage through after us, but because we find this is impossible we prefer to go back out again, rather than leaving the luggage behind.

But there's only one way we can get through, and that's by accepting that what we are going to is better value than all the clobber we have collected. Once we realise this we can say goodbye to it and leave it there outside while we walk quite easily into the life God has prepared for us.

Conflict

Explain that living the Christian life can sometimes feel rather like coping with an assault course. Ask for some volunteers to help you set up some obstacles in a central aisle. There may be a heavy groundsheet for crawling under, chairs or a small stepladder to climb over, a dustbin sack to jump in and some thick gloves to put on before using a knife and fork with which to eat a mini Mars or a few Smarties.

You will also need someone to run the course during the talk.

Remind everyone of how Joseph was treated by his brothers. Could he have avoided that? Perhaps he could have been more tactful earlier on, but now he couldn't really avoid the conflict and had to just go through it. (The volunteer goes under the groundsheet.)

What about Jesus; could he have avoided the conflict and pain of being crucified? What did he pray for in Gethsemane?

He certainly asked if he needn't go through with it (the volunteer goes round the climbing obstacle) but he didn't get a 'yes' answer to that prayer. Going through that agony and carrying on loving those who were killing him was the only way Jesus could save the world. So he did it. (The volunteer goes over the obstacle.)

What about us? Suppose there's a fight going on in the playground or on the underground. Can we avoid the conflict or do we have to get involved? It's probably wisest to avoid it (the volunteer walks round the dustbin bag) because it could make matters worse and we might get badly hurt. But suppose you are living in a country where you will be imprisoned unless you deny your faith in Christ. Can you avoid the conflict? (Ask the volunteer to put on the gloves and try eating with the knife and fork.) Answering this question honestly is as difficult as what the volunteer is doing – we need to pray urgently for those who are in this position, that they might be given the strength and courage to do God's will even when it is full of danger.

Treasure in clay pots

Bring along a piggy bank and some money to put in it. Some people keep their treasure safe in one of these, adding to it each week. (Drop some more money in.) Sometimes people will get an ordinary jar and fill it up with coins, so that soon it's full of treasure. The pot or jar is often very ordinary – it's the treasure inside which makes it special. People in Roman times used to use clay pots to keep their silver jewellery safe – archaeologists have found them, still guarding their treasure!

In one of the letters St Paul wrote, he said he thought we were all a bit like clay pots holding special treasure (see 2 Corinthians 4:7). As people we're just ordinary, but we've got something as Christians which is extraordinary – real treasure. It's being friends with God through Jesus which changes our lives from being ordinary to extra-special, because we're actually holding in us the love of the living God.

What does that look like?

We see a bit of what it looks like in Mark 3:1-6. Jesus notices a man whose arm is withered and shrunk so he can't use it, and immediately his heart goes out to that man, and more than anything he wants to set the man's arm free to wave and lift things, touch and hold things. His love for the man makes Jesus sad for him having to struggle, and he sets about mending him.

What Jesus doesn't do is look at the man and think, 'Ah yes, a man with an arm which doesn't work. But it's the Sabbath, so that's too bad; he'll have to stay like that – I'm not going to break the rules and heal him today.'

Well, of course he wouldn't think like that, because you can't be full of God's love and yet shut off your compassion. What Jesus did was the Godly, loving thing – he used his power of healing and set that man free, there and then, rules or no rules. And that offended the teachers of the Law. They had become so keen to keep the Law that they'd actually blocked God's light out, and couldn't see that Jesus was keeping the real spirit of the Law completely – love God and love one another.

So here we are as ordinary human pots, holding in us the light of God, and that's going to affect the way we live. We'll have to reach out in love and mercy to those around us, and that might mean we end up offending some people. But who cares? If we're living God's way, then we won't be offending God, and if living that way makes us unpopular sometimes, we'll be in very good company.

Why?

Begin by asking various people 'Why?' questions to which they have probably got logical answers. (For instance, 'Why are you wearing a scout uniform?'; 'Why do you wear glasses?'; 'Why are you sitting down?') Young children are always asking 'Why?' (Why?) Because as humans we want to make sense of the life we find ourselves in. When we understand why something happens we feel more comfortable with it – more in control.

But some questions are much harder to answer. (Like, 'Why does the sky look blue?') Only clever, knowledgeable people can answer those kinds of questions. Some questions we can't even answer from research in the library or years at college, because they aren't head knowledge but heart knowledge. (For instance, 'Why do you love someone?' and 'Why did that young person have to die?')

There must have been people at the crucifixion who were asking 'Why?'. Those who had known Jesus healing people and loving them may well have been those who were most disappointed to see him refusing to save himself. Perhaps they felt frustrated that he wasn't doing anything to get out of the pain.

It may be that we can't see the point of some dreadful tragedy in our own or someone else's life, and our hurt makes us sneer at God: 'If you were really a God of love you'd prevent this or sort it out.'

Jesus on the cross shows us that he stays with us in the agony of the hurt, and will in some way, which we don't yet understand, bring good and new life from it.

Courage

Begin by daring some volunteers to do various things, such as singing a nursery rhyme on their own, walking round the church blindfolded, or putting their hands into a bowl of custard.

Ask how many who are at school may be laughed at or teased for coming to church. (This is very common in many areas.) Encourage these people by recognising that they have been daring to come here today. Anyone who is teased or insulted at home or school or work for being a Christian is being brave, and Jesus knows all about their courage.

The truth is that if we are not being ridiculed, or meeting any conflict, it probably means we aren't living dangerously enough. Perhaps we've only got other Christians as our friends; perhaps we have arranged our hobbies and work so as to enjoy a peaceful life well away from anything challenging.

If so, we need to look at Jesus, and be prepared to make friends with someone who could do with some friendship but isn't well-liked; or perhaps we need to check that our nice peaceful life isn't making us complacent – perhaps it needs shaking up a bit.

The armour of prayer

Bring along various items of protective clothing: marigold gloves, a cycle helmet, wellington boots, a surgeon's mask and some earplugs. Demonstrate these items with volunteers, and explain how prayer is a protection against evil.

Nehemiah and the returned exiles needed protection against invaders while they rebuilt the walls of the city of Jerusalem (Nehemiah 4:6-15). As we are involved with the building of God's kingdom we shall find those who scoff and ridicule what we are doing, those who deliberately break down where we are building up, and others who can take us by surprise and discourage or destroy. Praying keeps the channels open between us and God, so that he can supply us with all the protective spiritual clothing we need.

Singing when things go wrong

Beforehand collect together several scummy-looking cartons, and label them with such things as 'Bitter disappointment', 'Unfair criticism', 'Severe irritation', and 'Personal failure'. Also provide lots of dried flowers, stickers, coloured paper, scissors and glue.

Begin by talking through the Paul and Silas story in Acts 16:16-40, pointing out their unexpected reaction to a very nasty state of affairs. Then show everyone the boxes which represent those awful times we sometimes get when the very last thing we'd think of doing would be praising God or singing. We feel perhaps that it wouldn't be honest if we did.

Ask some people to use the materials you have provided to make the boxes beautiful – without actually mending the boxes at all. While they work, talk about how some terrible circumstances are beyond our control and we can't change them; like when the train we need to catch is cancelled, when we have to live with a relative who drives us crazy, or when we don't get the grades we have worked so hard for. They are like Paul and Silas' prison, or like these boxes. If we can fill those times with praise, those awful situations will become beautiful. It's not a question of pretending that we're happy and that everything's wonderful – that would be ridiculous. It's a question of getting in touch with God, feeling, with him, the horror or ugliness of the situation and then deciding to praise him exactly where you are, which may well be through your tears. That is honest praise, praise that recognises God's beauty and his presence in the dreadful as well as the easy, the painful as well as the uplifting.

Try it next time you miss the bus, get let down by a friend or the washing machine pours filthy water all over the floor, and make those desolate places beautiful.

Have the finished boxes placed around the church to remind people.

Holding on to Jesus

Beforehand, beg or borrow a ballet student or two from a local dance school and ask them to work out a short routine of exercises at the barre.

Begin by introducing the students, and starting the exercise routine at the barre. Then interview them, to find out about why they need the barre there.

As Christians we learn about all sorts of difficult rules to live up to in our lives, and if we try them on our own we'll probably wobble all over the place and fall right over.

But Jesus is saying that he understands that; he knows we will need something to hold on to for support, and he isn't expecting us to be out there on our own.

New life in Christ means having Christ and his strength to hang on to during the difficult times each day when it's very hard to do what is right.

Ask the dancers to do one of the barre exercises again as everyone thinks of something they find hard to do in God's way – like always telling the truth, talking about people behind their backs without being critical, noticing jobs that need doing or spending money wisely – and remembers to use the 'barre' of God's love and firm support next time.

Spiritual fitness

Begin by having pre-arranged people to set up a fitness training course in the centre aisle. This needs to be done quickly and efficiently, as if it is all part of the training session. It only needs to be very simple – perhaps a skipping rope in one place, a step or box at another, and a small mat somewhere else. Have three volunteers, of mixed ages, and ask each to jog to one of the positions. They are going to do circuit training, skipping with the rope, stepping on and off the box and doing sit-ups on the mat. Start the stopwatch and move them on to the next activity after 20 seconds so that they have all completed the circuit in one minute.

Why do people do things like this? To get fit/have healthy bodies. What might happen if you weren't fit and rushed straight into a game of squash or football? You may get an injury, or even have a heart attack. We need to train to be fit before the big match, not after it.

We know that so well, and yet we sometimes expect to cope with very difficult and challenging problems in our lives without bothering to get spiritually fit first. What might our training circuit look like for getting spiritually fit?

Incorporate the ideas people suggest, which will no doubt include reading the Bible, praying/listening and serving others. Put a small group of people reading a Bible and commentaries suitable for different ages at one place, someone praying at another place, someone with a towel, jug of water and a basin at another.

If we get cracking on this daily circuit training, we will be making sure we're spiritually fitter and better equipped to face whatever the day throws at us.

Don't just say it, do it!

Beforehand arrange two small tables to be available during the talk, each with a mixing bowl and spoon, bag of peanuts, bag of raisins and bag of chocolate chips. Also arrange for someone to read out the recipe, one step at a time. Stand at one of the tables, and ask for a couple of volunteers to stand at the other table. Explain that you're fond of nutritious snacks, and are really keen to make one this morning. Introduce the person who will read out the recipe so that we all know what to do. As the steps are read out, encourage the volunteers to do what is said, but don't actually do them yourself – just keep babbling on about how good the recipe is, and how clear, and how you understand just what it means, etc.

When the snack is complete, let the volunteers show what it looks like and taste it. Now show your bowl, and let some of the younger children tell you that you haven't made anything at all. Protest that you must have done, because you had all the ingredients, and you listened to the recipe, and really agreed with it all. So what went wrong? The others heard what to do and did something about it; you didn't act on what you heard, so it wasn't really much good to anyone.

If we say we love God, but don't put that faith into action, our lives will end up as empty as that bowl.

Hear and obey

Beforehand get a box or case with a lock, and put a Bible in it. Lock it up and give the key to someone sitting on the end of a row, asking them to hold it out discreetly on the palm of their hand during the talk.

Begin by asking everyone to stand up, and then sit down again with their eyes fixed on you. They will just have demonstrated their faith in the chair still being there, because they were prepared to sit down without checking that the chair hadn't disappeared.

Give someone an instruction to go to the back of the church. When they get there they find a box which they can't open. Ask them to come back to the front, explaining as they do so that this is how we often act; we hear God's first calling or instruction and then stop listening or looking. Explain the root meaning of obedience (instant and alert listening) and send them off again, reminding them to be alert, listening and looking, as they go. This time they will probably notice the key (reminding them to look, if they seem to be ignoring it) and can open the box. Explain how God keeps in touch all the way, if only we will be alert to what he is saying through events around us. When the box is opened the Bible is found. That's another way God speaks to us and helps us, but it only works if we read it!

We need to keep in constant touch with God; if we aren't, it probably means we don't reckon much to God's power, and don't think he's worth taking seriously.

Receiving God's gifts

You will need:
A few books – a mixture of popular and little known
A Bible
An iPod
A first-aid box containing
some ointment labelled 'encouragement cream'
a bottle of 'refreshment'
a bandage labelled 'understanding'
an eye bath labelled 'grace to forgive'
a Bible labelled 'handbook'.

The first-aid box is wrapped like a present.

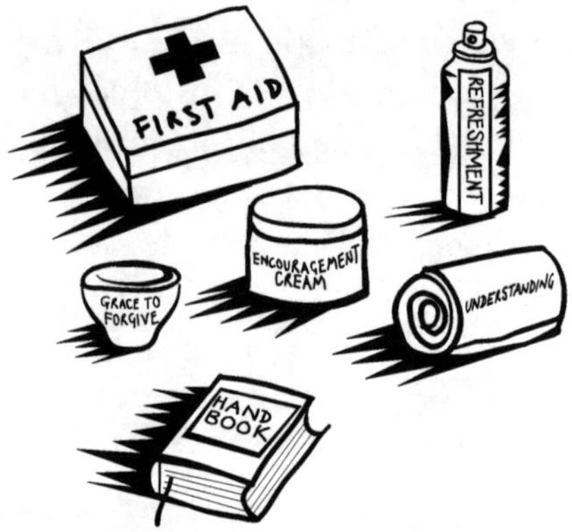

Begin by showing everyone some books. Involve their response – 'Do you like this one? . . . dislike that one?' When there is one they don't know whether they like or dislike, draw out the fact that they can't tell you because they haven't read it. Show the Bible – lots of people have one of these in their homes, but if we don't read it, it's as if we haven't got one.

Now ask for a willing helper and fit them up with the iPod, switching it on. Try to go on talking to them, but of course they won't be able to hear you. That's what happens to us – we don't hear God because we block out what he is trying to say to us and sometimes even accuse him of not speaking in our age. But if we really want to hear him, we've got to listen exclusively to him for at least some time every day. (Turn off iPod and release volunteer.)

And when we do read or hear God's word, what then? If we just put it away in a safe place and don't put it into practice, it will be just as if we haven't received anything. (Ask someone to offer you the present.) When they give it to you say 'thanks' but don't open it because it's too special. How does the giver feel when we do this? It hurts the giver and the present is no use to us, so he/she might as well give it to someone else. (Get him/her to do so.) Now this person opens it up and let's have a look at what's inside. (Go through the different items together, remarking how useful it would have been and how it's exactly what you needed.) So . . . make good use of what God offers – read his word, listen to him in prayer and put what you receive into action.

Natural Christians

First of all give some examples of how things happen naturally. Put some sugar in a drink and it can't help tasting sweet; have a brace clamped to your teeth and they can't help growing straight. Mix blue and yellow and you can't help making green. (All these can be actually watched if you wish – all those with braces can come out together and flash a silver smile.)

This principle works for bad things as well as good. If you drink 16 pints of lager you can't help getting drunk; if you put on skunk perfume you can't help smelling of skunk.

Since this is so, we will need to be loving people in order to behave in a loving way; we will have to be dedicated to serving God and others if we are to be able to act with God's character. Whatever kind of people we are on the inside will naturally show in the way we behave on the outside, so rather than working on doing things we think will impress people, God is inviting us to work with him in a transforming process from the inside – he can make us the kind of people who naturally think and love unselfishly, and enjoy our lives all the more for it.

The Christian adventure

Begin by asking about some of the adventures people have had, so that they share them around. (Just one-liners, like 'I was trapped in a lift once'; 'I got dragged along by a runaway horse', etc.) Have a collection of adventure stories, including books that every age group will recognise, and have amongst the collection the Bible, and *Pilgrim's Progress.* Read snippets of exciting bits from the books, including 2 Corinthians 11:25-27. Point out how Paul wasn't really the James Bond type, but as he went around telling people about Jesus' love for them, the adventures seemed to come and meet him!

That may already have happened to some people in this congregation. They may have mentioned Jesus and been teased at school, or insulted at work or at home because of it. When that happens, we shouldn't let it put us off – it's actually an exciting sign that we're on the right track, and are involved in an adventure story. Try writing it down, praying lots for people involved, and wait and see how God works in them. The Christian adventure is exciting, can be dangerous and should probably carry a government health warning! Try it.

Perseverance

If possible, beg or borrow a cycling or rowing machine, but don't worry if this is impractical.

Start by showing someone having a workout on the machine, gradually increasing the resistance to make it harder work. If you aren't using a machine, have people skipping without stopping, or doing sit-ups. As they work, point out how in order to get fit we put in a lot of effort, and when the going gets difficult, we struggle on, and put up with it, because we consider the effort worth while.

Let the volunteers have a rest and explain how we are also called to endure things in our Christian life. This may mean the daily effort to get on with someone in our family whom we find difficult; the constant battle against temptation of some sort; the regular, tiring care of someone who depends on us. Often the nasty part is not having any idea when this difficult part of our life will end, and if that gets us down, we are better off thinking just of today, or even just for this moment. God loves us, and will not let us suffer on and on in our own strength. He will be right there, providing exactly what we need to cope with the situation. And one last thing: God has promised us that we will never be tempted beyond our endurance, and there will always be an escape route if necessary.

All the way through

Beforehand, get two sticks of rock which have a name going all the way through them. If you find these impossible to get hold of, use two Swiss rolls instead.

Begin by showing everyone a stick of rock and get someone to read what it says at the top. Break a piece off and give it to them. Surprise, surprise, it still says the same thing! Break this piece off and so on, until all the rock is given away, and we have found that the writing is there all the time, through every part of the rock.

Now remind everyone of Jeremiah being thrown down the well and left for dead (Jeremiah 38:1-13). Before he went down he was telling the people God's message. Even when they pull him up, he's still telling the people God's message. (Doesn't give up easily, does he?) He's like the piece of rock (show the unbroken one), keeping to God's message all the way through, during the good times, the dangerous times and the painful times.

What about us? Are we God's friends just at the beginning, when we're all excited by the faith, or have just been baptised or confirmed? Or are we still God's friends when we get into trouble? (Snap off a piece of rock.) When everything is going really well for us? (Snap.) When life is full of pressures? (Snap.) When our friends aren't interested? (Snap.) If we are real friends of Jesus, we will stay his friends all the way through.

Waiting in hope

Beforehand, get a kitchen timer, and one of those automatic timers which you fix on a lamp.

Begin by explaining how you are going to set the timer for *X* minutes, at which time the talk should be finishing. You are also setting the light to come on half-way through the talk. (Do this.)

Talk about the way things seem to take ages coming, because we want them so much – like birthdays, Christmas, holidays, pension day or tea time. Other things seem to come too fast – like telephone bills, exams or dentist appointments – because we aren't looking forward to them at all.

The early Christians were really looking forward to Jesus coming back in glory, and it seemed to be taking for ever. People who expected it to happen before they were 16, grew to 75 and died, and still Jesus hadn't come. It has been about 2000 years now, and he still hasn't come.

Now as soon as we start measuring the time for something, it seems to make us impatient. 'A watched pot never boils', they say. Because you know this talk will end when the ringer goes, you are probably all waiting for it to ring at any moment, especially as the light will remind you that it's all being timed. Peter told the people not to think God was slow in coming; he was just patiently waiting for the right time, and that might be any time. That's still true – Jesus could come again at any moment, on any day. All we know for certain is that he is definitely going to return in glory, and we can't give an exact time and date to it. Meanwhile, we can live our lives to the full, living the life of love that God shows us, and keeping in close contact with him through prayer and worship, so that we are ready when he does appear.

Citizens of heaven

If you have anyone in uniform present, ask them to come to the front, one each of various sorts of uniform, such as a choir member, a cub or brownie. They can sit down, and when you mention an activity they might expect to do, they stand up. Sometimes several people will be standing up and at other times only one person.

Explain how we do expect to behave in particular ways – even if we're not wearing uniform. Car drivers need to behave as a responsible people, for instance, or they might be a danger to themselves and others.

Every citizen is expected to act reasonably, and keep to the country's laws, so that life is safer for everybody. We are citizens twice over (twinned citizens, rather than twinned cities) because we are citizens of our earthly city of Bromsgrove or Plymouth, and also citizens of heaven. So we have to make sure we behave like citizens of the kingdom of heaven, and be quite strict with ourselves about this, working at the parts we find hard and exercising the parts we manage more easily.

Our heavenly home

First show some colourful travel brochures, reading out snippets from them, and then talk about how nice it is to go home after a holiday, because home, for most people, is very special.

Ask everyone to think of the first home they remember. Imagine walking up to the front door, and looking in the rooms that they may not have visited in their imagination for a long time, or that they may have left this morning. Take them through various rooms, drawing their attention to things like the furniture, the kitchen window and so on, which will help bring their memories flooding back. That was the home they started out from on a journey which has brought them to Sunday morning, and the particular pew they are sitting in. Heaven is our spiritual home, and although we don't know any details, like the furniture and the windows of our earthly homes, we do know that it is a place of deep happiness and fulfilment, free from all tears and anxieties, lit with love and contentment. (Sounds good, doesn't it?)

If this was on a holiday programme, they may well be waiting now to hear the bad news of how expensive it is to go there, and how little chance ordinary people have of getting in. The wonderful news is that Jesus has already paid for us to go, and the fare was death by crucifixion, with the sins of the world heavy on his shoulders. What is more, we are not counted as tourists, but citizens of heaven. If we choose to walk with Jesus, he will bring us safely through our own death journeys to live in heaven. If we want, heaven can be our home for the whole of eternity.

Right and wrong

For good or evil?

Bring along a kitchen knife, a pen or pencil, a can of paint spray and a £10 or £20 note. You will also need two signs, one saying 'Good' and the other 'Evil'.

Begin by observing that lots of things we handle every day can be used either for good or for evil. Ask for two volunteers to hold the signs, some distance apart, and go through each of the objects in turn, gathering from different people how each can be used. Take the objects to the appropriate notice for each suggestion.

Now ask a person to stand up. It's not only things which can be used for good or for evil; it's people as well. Stand the person beside the 'Evil' sign. In what ways can a person use themselves for evil? (Collect suggestions from people of all ages.) Stand the person by the 'Good' sign. In what ways can a person use themselves for good? (Collect suggestions.)

In James 3:9 we read about the tongue: 'We use it to give thanks to our Lord and Father and also to curse our fellow-man, who is created in the likeness of God.' We need to try and use our voices to encourage one another and help one another. We need to use our voices to tell out the truth, and not use the voices God has given us to spread unkind gossip, or lies, or to be rude and unkind.

In Romans 6:15-19 St Paul tells us that all the different parts of our bodies can either be offered to sin as instruments of evil, or offered to God as instruments of good. We've looked at our voices. What about our hands? Our minds? Our maleness or our femaleness? Our feet? Our ears? Suggest that during this week they make a point of checking how they are using all the parts of their body, and seeing if they offer all those parts of themselves to God for good.

Dead and alive

In Romans 6:1-11 St Paul tells us that we are to think of ourselves as dead to sin and alive to God through Christ Jesus. What does that mean?

Well, perhaps a few sleeping lions can help. Ask for a few volunteers to play 'sleeping lions' in the aisle, while you and some others try to get them to move. They have to remain as still as they possibly can. Point out that they have to think of themselves as 'asleep' to all those temptations to move which are going on around them. That is rather like us thinking of ourselves being dead to sin. We have to remind ourselves that sin is something which no longer concerns us or has any hold on us.

Ask a few people to say what noises there are in their home at night – any creaks or tickings or chimes. Then draw people's attention to the way we have no difficulty sleeping through these noises, because we know we don't have to worry about them. Some parents will have found that if it isn't your turn to get up and feed the baby you're quite likely to sleep through the crying. You are 'dead' to that sound because you know it isn't anything to do with you. And we are told that we are to think of ourselves as dead to sin.

But it isn't just being dead to sin – it's also being alive to God. What does that mean? Perhaps some people who like chocolate can help us here. Choose a few volunteers and tell them to stand with their backs to you and the congregation. When they think they can detect the presence of chocolate, tell them to raise their hand. Now, as you talk about the way we can always hear what we want to hear, start to open a bar of chocolate, and even though there isn't much sound, and they have their backs to you, it probably won't be very long before they notice, either by hearing or smelling, or both.

That's like us being 'alive' to God. We are going to live as dead to sin, but expectant and interested as far as God is concerned. We will be so tuned in to God that we notice his still, small voice, recognise him in all we see and in those we meet, and live with our hearts and ears and wills turned in his direction all through every day, whatever is going on around us.

The right time

Bring along a pot of jam, some toffee or fudge, a skipping rope and a camera. Talk about the importance of getting the timing right when you are making jam or toffee, skipping or taking a photo. Invite experts from the congregation to describe that 'right moment' and how you know when it's there and don't miss it. Sometimes we do miss the right moment and end up with solid stuff that won't spread and tastes of burnt saucepan, our legs tangled up in the rope, or a photo of a giraffe's bottom.

St Paul talks about Jesus being born 'when the time was right' (Galatians 4:4). That particular date in history – whenever it actually was – fitted in perfectly with God's rescue plan. And so he acted, and what we call Christmas happened: a baby was born who was God's own Son, and would grow up to show everyone what God is really like, in the language of being human, which we can all understand.

God is very good at knowing the right time to act. We can always trust him with that. Often he will bring things together in a way and at a time which brings blessing to many people rather than only one. Those who are older can look back over their lives and see how this has been true. We might have prayed for something to happen and got fed up with God not seeming to answer for ages. But later on we can see that the time of waiting perhaps helped us, or allowed something else important to happen, and God's timing turned out to be for the best.

Sometimes we don't understand God's sense of timing and would much prefer him to take our advice! Perhaps we are still feeling let down by God over something which we so wanted and has never happened. We need to remember that it is the God of all eternity that we worship, and it may be that we shall only understand when we get to heaven. We are a bit like bewildered pets at the vets who find their owners bringing them along to have a stranger poke needles into them; we don't understand why and just know that it hurts.

Jesus himself was not born into a comfortable home with an efficient maternity hospital just down the road. The family had to escape to another country before he was two years old, because King Herod wanted him killed. But still the time of his birth was right.

What God did was provide his Son with a human family to love him and look after him. When couples who love one another take on that commitment of marriage, and raise their children together, through all the inevitable strains and stresses, they are giving newborn children a wonderful, Godly gift. And as the Christian family here, we are all given one another to look after and be looked after by. Whatever our age, sex or marital state, we are all children together, born into God's family and enjoying God's own parenting, which is one thing in life we can really trust.

Making good

Beforehand, arrange for a local builder/decorator to be interviewed, preferably in working clothes and carrying his tools.

Introduce the guest, and ask his advice about a structural problem (either real or imagined). When the builder talks about the importance of all the 'making good', suggest that surely he could just smear some more plaster over the top, and wouldn't that be as good? Or put on thick wallpaper to hide the cracks? Let the builder explain what will eventually happen if the real problem isn't sorted out.

Thank the guest builder and have a couple of the children bring him a mug of tea as it's time for his tea break.

While the builder drinks his tea, explain how what is true for walls and windows is true for us as well. If we have been mean or a pain, or lazy, or if we've been telling lies or living lies, or if there is anything at all in the way we behave which is not right, loving and honest, then we are like a building with bad cracks and damp. As the builder told us, the only way to put it right is to have the wrong things cleared away, and then be built up soundly again.

God can do that in us if we want. He will help us put our lives right, however bad a state they are in. Tell him you are sorry you tell lies, and want to be more honest. He will help you become an honest person who others can trust. Tell God your sister / father-in-law / colleague winds you up and you hate all the rows and want to be more able to cope. God will help you improve those relationships. Tell God you find it hard to share your toys or your money, and want to be more generous. He will help you do it.

But we can't put anything right until we see that there is a problem. It was only when the damp and cracks were noticed that the builder was called in.

John the Baptist spoke about 'repentance'. That means, 'Look at your lives; see those cracks and damp patches; and get them sorted out.'

Keeping clean

Probably, quite a lot of us washed before we came out today. Why do we keep ourselves clean with regular washing? (Collect ideas and reasons.) Conclude that there are good reasons for washing. It's all to do with keeping healthy as well as being pleasant to sit next to! Mark 7:1-23 talks out what makes us unclean. If we are talking about our bodies, what sort of things make us unclean, or dirty? (Collect a few ideas.)

Now it was traditional for Jewish religious people to do lots and lots of washing. Some of this was to keep everything clean and healthy and, having lived as wandering nomads in hot desert country all that was very important. But there was another kind of 'being unclean' which wasn't to do with bodies but souls. Sin is your soul, or spiritual nature, being unclean and in need of a good cleanup. Jewish people believed that eating certain foods or not following special rituals would make you unclean.

But whereas it's outside things that make our bodies unclean and in need of washing, Jesus explained that with our souls it's thoughts and wants from deep inside us that often lead us into sin, making us unclean. Like what, for instance?

- Like when we have mean, unkind thoughts
- when we feel like hating or despising people because they've got what we want
- whenever we want what we know is wrong and against God's way of living
- when it seems like a clever idea to lie our way out of trouble
- when doing something unselfish seems too much like hard work and we can't be bothered with it.

When we are baptised, we're dunked in water, partly as a sign that we're being washed clean from sin. (And in some churches, the priest washes his hands just after the bread and wine are brought to the altar, as an outward sign that he wants God to wash him clean of sin, ready for this special part of the service.)

So if those wrong and bad thoughts and drives make us sin, so that our souls are unclean, how on earth can we get clean again? Can we scrub our souls with soap and water, or soak all our nastiness away in a hot bath?

No, we can't. But there is a way of getting our souls clean without leaving any stain of sin at all. It's a two-stage washing process, rather like putting stuff out for the laundry because we know it's dirty, and then having it washed clean. And it's called *repentance and forgiveness.*

Once we realise that our souls are messy and dirty with sin, and that makes us sad, we bring all of it to Jesus, tell him how sorry we are and how we would love our souls to be completely clean again. *That's repentance.*

What Jesus does is to take our souls and soak away all the sin in a wonderful bath of *forgiveness,* that leaves us feeling free and happy and spiritually clean.

Freed from the yoke

Out of strong card (or a wooden broom handle) make a demonstration yoke to show, on a brave volunteer, how conquerors used to subdue their captives. When you release the volunteer captive, talk to them about how good it feels to be free of the yoke.

In Isaiah 9:2-5 the prophet speaks about his people being freed from the yoke. At the time, the people he was speaking to were being threatened by another country. It looked as if Assyria might well come and yoke the people up as captives, and take them far away from their own homes and their temple and their country, to live in exile in the country of their conquerors.

Isaiah showed the people that if they went on turning away from him by treating the poor unfairly, and spoiling themselves while others starved, then God would not save them from this attack. They were already 'yoked' up as slaves to their greed and selfishness, and their worries about the Assyrians.

Through Isaiah the prophet, God spoke to his people. He told them that he loved them, and that he longed for them to sort their lives out and trust him again. God would then be able to look after them and keep them and their holy city of Jerusalem safe. It would be like their yokes being broken in pieces, so they would be completely free.

Show the demonstration yoke again on another volunteer. Do any of us wear invisible yokes and need to be set free? We may be wearing yokes of selfishness, or resentment; we may be always wishing for things we can't have. We may still feel guilty about something we did. We may need healing of some emotional damage which is holding us back from living freely.

Jesus came so that we could be set free from all these yokes. He's an expert 'yoke shatterer'! He's the kind of light that makes all the darkness in our lives and minds and hearts disappear. If we let him in to walk around our own lives, as well as the lake of Galilee, he will set us free from all those yokes that hold us captive. And then we'll be able to walk through life with a new spring in our step, full of hope.

Taking God's prize

Bring along the details of a children's colouring competition, and also one of those junk mail promotional letters which tell you that you have already been selected as a winner.

Begin by sharing this exciting letter with everyone, reading out some of the blurb, and getting a volunteer to scratch any secret messages included. No doubt many of us receive these kinds of letters. When we do so, we have a choice: are we going to bin it (or preferably recycle it), or will we take them up on their wonderful offer and claim our prize? What we decide will depend on all kinds of factors, such as how busy we are, how desperate for winnings we are, how many previous disappointments we have experienced, and whether we actually believe them.

But one thing is certain. Unless we decide to return our reply slip, we have no chance of winning anything at all. It's the same with colouring competitions. A prize is offered and anyone has a chance of winning. But if you don't get your felt-tips or paints out and do the colouring, and send it off in time, you will have no chance of winning a prize, however good you are at colouring.

Today we are being reminded by God that he has great prizes and gifts for us, which he longs for us to enjoy (see Philippians 3:14; 2 Timothy 4:8). He wants to see us all as winners, happily receiving the gift that has been reserved specially for us. But . . . and it is a big 'but' . . . unless we choose to turn to God and take him up on his offer, we will have no chance at all of winning. If we choose wrong instead of right, evil instead of good, and self instead of God, we cannot have the joy and peace and life that God longs to give us. We don't just get it anyway, however we live. Lots of people think that is what happens, but it isn't because God isn't like that. He is a God of goodness and love, truth and kindness. Do we want to go along with that? We have to choose it, then, and start doing something about it.

As soon as we choose it, God can give us all the help we need, and he will, because all he wants is for us to know complete and lasting happiness with him.

The law of love

Hold a large edition of the Bible, and tell everyone that today we are all going to read the whole lot as part of our talk!

Explain that Jesus once gave a summary of the whole of the Bible, in a couple of sentences. (Reader's Digest can eat their heart out!) He was saying that everything in all the law and the prophets was an exploring and working out of this. (Have Matthew 22:37-39 written out large, and invite everyone to join you in reading it out.) There – we've read the Bible! Or, to be more precise, we have read the subject matter of the whole Bible, because everything in it is to do with what we just read – people learning to love God with their whole being, and their neighbours as themselves. It's the story of their learning, their mistakes and failures, and of God's great love helping us make the impossible possible. (Well worth reading the full-length version!)

Let's look at what it means to love others as we love ourselves. How do we love ourselves? Invite a couple of friends to come and help show us. Get one to stand behind the other, with the front person putting their hands behind their back, and the back person providing them with substitute arms by pushing their own arms through the front person's. Have someone offer them a wrapped chocolate which they can eat, and give them a brush so they can do their hair.

All day long we look after ourselves like this, feeding and washing and scratching ourselves whenever the need arises. Even if we don't admit to loving ourselves our actions show that we do. If we start getting too hot, our body kindly makes us sweat to cool us down. If we're threatened by the cold, our helpful body sets us shivering and raises our hairs to warm us up again. And if there's a real emergency (the children can make an ambulance siren sound), the body shuts down some systems and kicks in with others to keep us alive as long as possible. That's love for you!

So if we are to love others like that, we'll be attentive, looking out for one another's well-being and ready to help when we see someone in need. We'll be doing what we can to feed the hungry and look after those with problems. We'll scratch where it itches but not where it doesn't. We'll be ready to drop everything and be there for people if there's an emergency and they need us. We'll do everything we can to help them feel better and get through the difficult times.

And where does all this love come from? From our wonderful God, who made us all in the first place, and loves to see all his children caring for one another like this.

Good news – bad news

Bring along some advertisements proclaiming special offers which look like absolutely wonderful bargains, and completely good news, but when you read the small print you find all sorts of extra bad news which makes the bargain not quite so fantastic as it first sounded. (For example: '£50 OFF!' – when you spend £300; 'Children go free!' – but only if you travel after 10 o'clock and buy two full adult fares.) Of course, those who designed the advertisement hope that by the time you've read the small print you are so keen to take them up on the offer that you will be prepared to go along with the extra requirements.

Jesus is never like that with us; he is always completely open and honest. Jesus always gives us both the good and the bad news, gently but firmly, because he loves and respects us. That's why we know that we can trust him absolutely. (At this point you could have two people acting out the following conversation.) Jasmin and Mel are in a dress shop. Jasmin is trying various clothes against herself.

Jasmin What about this, Mel? What d'you think?

Mel Yeah, that's cool.

Jasmin Or this one?

Mel Yeah, great!

Jasmin There's this one as well . . .

Mel Yeah, fantastic!

Jasmin Oh, come on, Mel, they can't all look brilliant. Tell me what you really think.

Mel OK. I think they all make you look old.

Jasmin *(cross)* Oh, nice! I thought you were my friend! *(walks out of shop, calling back to Mel)* Anyway, you've got as much fashion sense as a woolly vest!

Mel *(shrugs)* Thought she wanted me to be honest.

If someone is always saying how wonderful we are, even when we know very well that we have not been at all wonderful, we can't really trust that they are telling us the truth. But if someone tells us the bad news when it's bad and the good news when it's good, then we know we can trust them to be honest with us.

In Mark 8:31-38 we find the disciples expecting something that can't happen. They are thinking that, as Jesus is the Messiah, he is one day going to lead an army to drive out the Romans from their country. Jesus takes the risk of them rejecting him, and being angry and disappointed, rather than lead them into false hopes. In effect he's saying, 'OK, so you know I'm the Messiah, but I'm afraid I'm not going to be the kind of Messiah you're all expecting. It's not going to look like a great victory at first – it's going to look like complete failure.' Jesus tells them he's going to be killed, all as part of his work as Messiah.

And Peter can't bear to hear this 'bad news'. He tries to shut it out and persuade Jesus that he must be mistaken. Sometimes we do the same. Perhaps Jesus nudges us to give something up, or change something in our lives, or make friends with someone we don't want to, and we spend a lot of time and energy pretending not to hear, or pretending that God must be mistaken. He isn't mistaken; he's just being lovingly honest with us, and we take it as bad news because we don't want to hear it as the truth.

We've reached the second week of Lent, our thoughtful time in the desert. Let's use the coming week to take notice when Jesus nudges us, and go along with what he suggests, even if it means giving up something we like doing.

Rules

Talk about some of the rules we are given, such as, 'Wear your seatbelt', 'Don't lean out of the window on a moving train', 'Don't play on the railway line' or 'Don't keep poisons in old lemonade bottles'. Gather ideas about why they are good, sensible rules which are worth keeping. Point out that they are good rules whether we actually know the reasons or not.

Now ask for some volunteers to stand around as trees in the garden of the story from Genesis (see Genesis 2:15-17 and 3:1-7). Give the volunteers real or paper fruits to hold. God's rule for Adam and Eve was 'Don't eat fruit from this tree'. Hang this rule round the tree in the centre of the garden. Now God has very good reasons for making this rule, based on his love for Adam and Eve and his concern for them. And since God is God, that rule is the most important thing for Adam and Eve to remember. However tasty the fruit looks, whatever they may be told it will do to help them, they are always to keep hold of God's rule (what was it?) and stick to keeping that. Anything that cuts across God's rule must be wrong.

Ask two people who think they will be able to keep to God's rule without disobeying it. These two are going to be Adam and Eve. Show them how tasty the fruit looks and try to persuade them to try it. Tell them that it will do wonderful things for them, and make them wise like God. When they (hopefully) manage to resist the temptation to do what God's rule told them not to, praise them, and then point out that they managed it this time, but we are always being tempted to be disobedient to God's rule of love, and when it next happens we need to stick close to God, and remember his rule: 'Love God and love one another'.

Adam and Eve in the story stand for all of us who are human. And humans tend not to be very good at resisting temptation. God loves us and understands what it is like to be humans being tempted. We know that because Jesus was tempted during his life on earth. He will give us the strength we need to resist those pressures of temptation, but that doesn't mean it's going to be easy. Resisting temptation is *very hard*, and that's why Jesus told us to pray about it every day of our life: 'Lead us not into temptation but deliver us from evil.' Let's use the strength God offers; we need all the help we can get!

Free to obey

Borrow a toy farm set, or a playmat with animals, houses and cars to arrange on it. Also borrow a remote control vehicle.

Set the youngest children arranging their landscape in a space where they can be seen. Then have the remote control vehicle demonstrated in the aisle. As it is directed to run in different directions, talk about the kind of control the demonstrator has over the vehicle; the vehicle has no choice in the matter. Look at the kind of control demonstrated in the children arranging the animals and buildings. Here, too, they are deciding for the animals what is the best place for them to be. These decisions may be sensitive and based on what the animals would probably like best, but still they have no choice, and must remain in the pond or looking over a fence where they are placed, unless the children decide they need a change.

What about our behaviour in this service? We mostly all sit/stand/kneel in all the right places very obediently, though no one can make us join in attentively if we choose not to, and we could, of course, choose to be very disruptive and spoil it for others.

The Bible tells us that God cared about the people he made. As soon as Adam was made he was invited to help God and share in his work (see Genesis 2:15). God would bring the animals to Adam, and Adam named them (see Genesis 2:18-20). (Take some pictures or animal models to the children and let them name them.) The gardening was not drudgery, but wholesome and rewarding work, with God and people working together.

This is a picture of us all living in harmony with God, obeying him, and living as he suggests is right and good for us. It isn't remote control, with God making us do what he wants. It isn't God doing what is best for us whether we want the best or not. It is God loving us and inviting us to work with him. He lets us choose whether to live this way or not. He hopes we will choose what he knows will make us really deep-down happy, but if we choose ways that mess things up for us or others, he won't stop us. He will just be there ready to dry our tears and help us try again when we realise how foolish we have been.

The right point of view

Begin by drawing attention to the direction everyone is facing in church. Obviously this will vary according to your architecture and the age of the building. The architecture reflects a focus and a general direction which the planners thought of most importance. Perhaps if you were all about to start planning from scratch, you might arrange things slightly differently!

Once you have established the general seating focus, move to another part of the church, such as the entrance. If people are going to continue facing you, they will all have to turn round. That is because at the moment the important thing going on is you speaking, and that takes over in importance from the general focus of the building.

Now move somewhere else so that everyone has to turn round again. In Matthew 5:17-48 Jesus taught about the Law, which is summed up in the ten commandments. Have these displayed on card, or on a screen, or walk to the part of the church where they are written on the wall. They are good rules to live by and our whole law system is still based on them. But with all rules there is a problem. Jesus wanted his followers (and that includes us) to remember that the really important thing is to stay focused on God in everything we do.

You may have never killed anyone, but the spirit of the law means more than that, just as our focus is more than just sitting facing the front. It also means making sure we haven't got unkind or destructive thoughts about people, that we're not making people feel stupid or useless, that we aren't putting other people down or running them down behind their backs, because those things are in the destructive spirit of hate, which is the opposite of God's law of love. As you mention each of these, move around the building so people have to move their 'attitudes' to see you.

What we need to do is keep our eyes fixed on Jesus, and whatever we are doing we can think to ourselves, 'Does this thing I'm doing or saying or thinking make Jesus happy? Is it a loving thing to do or think or say?'

And if it is, carry on. If it isn't, stop and change direction.

Like salt and light

You will need a large saucepan, a pack of spaghetti, a jar of Italian sauce and a large carton of salt, a jug, a teacup and a tablespoon. You will also need a table lamp and a bright spotlight.

Produce the first set of items, setting them out and talking about cooking pasta. Invite a good cook from the congregation to supervise! Explain that the best cookery books say that pasta can't be seasoned after it's cooked, so we need to add the salt to the cooking water. Pick up the salt, and wonder aloud how much salt to use. A jugful? Get the cook to explain what would happen if you put in that much salt. A teacupful? Still too much! A tablespoonful? Still too much. If we use that much all we will taste is the salt, and the whole idea of salt is that it isn't really noticed but brings out the flavour of the other ingredients.

That's what we are called to do as Christians (see Matthew 5:13): not to take over and dominate or possess people, or want to control them, but in humility to make ourselves available and useful in helping to give other people the freedom and the confidence to be themselves. That may mean more listening and less speaking; it may mean being less concerned about being thought important and more concerned about other people's needs being recognised. It is the way of quiet, loving service.

Now flash the spotlight around so that it goes in people's eyes (but don't overdo this!). Explain that Jesus also calls us to be light (see Matthew 5:14-16). That doesn't mean trying to blind people with our natural brilliance, or trying subtly to impress others, so that we're more like disco lights, designed for a flashy effect. The kind of light we are called to be is a much more practical sort, rather like a table lamp, perhaps, which simply helps people to see better, so they don't bump into things and hurt themselves, and so they can get on with living more effectively.

Salt and light are just simple things, but they are things which can make a great difference. As Christians we are called to be like that – just our ordinary selves, but through our faith in God, able to make a difference.

Loving our enemies

Beforehand, ask the children to make lots of paper chains.

Remind everyone that Jesus teaches us to love our enemies and forgive those who sin against us (see Luke 6:27-36). How on earth are we supposed to do it? Surely enemies are people you hate? Why does Jesus tell us to love them, then?

Ask a volunteer to run and skip around a bit and talk about how life can feel when we are happy with ourselves, and everything is going well for us. But sooner or later we get into a mood with someone, someone upsets us and annoys us, someone else winds us up, someone makes our life a real misery, someone lets us down and spoils our plans, someone hurts a person we love, or someone steals from us a close friend or a marriage partner, or our dignity in old age. (At each suggestion, drape a chain around the volunteer until s/he is smothered in chains.) And if we haven't forgiven these people who have sinned against us and hurt us, we end up still carrying invisible chains which weigh us down. The volunteer can walk around bowed down with the heavy chains.

So when Jesus says to us, 'Love your enemies and forgive those who wrong you', he knows it is hard, but he also knows it will set us free to live fully again. Every time we say (and really mean it), 'I forgive you for what you did', a chain drops off. (Pull a chain off the volunteer.) Every time we wrestle with our feelings of hate for someone and ask God to help us sort things out, a chain drops off. (Pull off another chain.) Pull off the remaining chains, with everyone saying 'I forgive you!' for each one.

Jesus doesn't like to see us weighed down with heavy invisible chains of hate and resentment and bitterness against people. He wants us to be free to enjoy life, and he will always help us to do the forgiving. Forgiving is not easy; it's very hard work. If you know there is someone you are finding it very hard to forgive, ask God for the grace to forgive and then work at the forgiving. Don't live with the chains any more.

Shining

You will need a hand mirror.

Begin by asking everyone if they have noticed how people often look like their pets, particularly dogs! Perhaps they choose a pet which reflects their own character. Today we are looking at how spending our lives with God makes us more and more like him.

Use the mirror to catch the light and throw it on to people's faces. Mirrors are excellent at spreading light around, because they are able to reflect light. Moses, who was a close friend of God was the person who led the people of Israel out of Egypt, where they had been slaves, and through the desert to the promised land. When Moses had been on a mountain in God's company and was given the Ten Commandments, he came down from the mountain with his face glowing and radiant. Like a mirror, he was reflecting some of the glory of God (see Exodus 34:29-35). Sometimes if people are really happy – a bride and bridegroom getting married to the one they love, students hearing they have passed all their exams really well, or children on their birthday – we talk about them looking radiant, or glowing with happiness. How we are feeling and thinking inside changes the way we look.

When Jesus was on earth, three of his close friends were on a mountain with him when he was praying, and they saw him not just with a radiant face, but completely shining, or transfigured (see Luke 9:28-36). What they were seeing was the glory of God in Jesus, who was and is completely at one with God, his Father. They heard God's voice explaining who Jesus was and telling them to listen to him. Not like listening to music in the background, but really attentive listening, like you would listen to instructions for flying an aeroplane if you were the only person on board able to bring it safely to land.

When we live our lives close to Jesus like this, listening to his quiet voice guiding us, talking over our problems and happiness with him, and working at living a good life, then gradually our faces will start to show some of God's glory, and our lives will start to shine, reflecting God's loving nature like mirrors (flash the light again) reflecting the light.

Tasters of heaven

Bring along some tasters of a particular cheese, tiny chunks such as those you find in most supermarkets from time to time. Bring also a block of the same cheese, labelled.

Show your tray of tasters for the cheese you have brought to recommend. Suggest that people try a taster of it to see whether they like it. Since these tasters came off the main block of cheese, you can guarantee that they will taste as good as the main block. Discuss their findings briefly.

Although we haven't been to heaven, God gives us lots of little 'tasters' which help us find out what it is like. Whenever we sense Jesus giving us peace of mind or joy, or the lovely knowledge that God really loves and cares for us, we are getting a taster of life after death. Jesus lives in heaven so when he comes into us, he doesn't leave heaven behind but brings it with him. So the more we live in God's company and follow Jesus, the more of heaven we will have in our lives even before we die.

Explain that lots of people think Christians are crazy believing that there is life after death. Since they can't see beyond death, they don't think there can be anything like heaven. If I had never seen the yellow daffodil flowers in spring, I would probably think people were crazy burying dry bulbs in their earth at this time of year. But because I have seen what happens to those bulbs, I trust that they won't just rot in the ground. If I were a caterpillar, I would probably laugh at anyone suggesting that one day I would be flying about with colourful wings. It isn't true that the only real things are those we can see.

It is sometimes difficult to trust that what we can't see is still there, but we make the effort to do it whenever we drive in fog, walk along looking around instead of at the path under our feet, or wash our backs. So it is quite possible. And Jesus has told us that there really is life after death, and lots of people saw him alive after he had died. So we aren't crazy for believing there is life after death; we happen to know it's true, and we've already tasted little bits of how lovely it is.

The right image

Bring in an ordinary mirror. Also make a distorting mirror using a sheet of very shining wrapping paper. It can either be stuck on bent card or simply held by two volunteers. Invite a few people to see themselves in both mirrors, or walk the mirrors round the church reflecting people here and there. Which reflection looks most like them?

Sometimes we are like good mirrors, whenever we reflect God's loving by being loving to others. Or we may reflect God's forgiving nature when we forgive someone who has been unkind to us. Or we may reflect God's faithfulness when we are trustworthy ourselves.

But sometimes we are like bad mirrors. We distort loving into possessiveness; we distort relaxing into laziness; we distort honesty into critical gossip; or pleasure into greed. Worst of all, we distort trust. We are designed to trust God, and when we trust in things and people instead of God, our lives get twisted and misshapen.

If we get our trust in the right place, everything else will start reflecting properly and our lives will be very beautiful and very fulfilling.

Treasure hunt

Beforehand, prepare three treasure maps of the building with an X marking the spot where the treasure is to be found. All three maps have the treasure in a different place. Where the first map leads, have a locked box with a bread roll in it. Where the second leads, have a locked box with a T-shirt in it, and where the third map leads, have a large bunch of keys, which includes the (marked) keys to the other two boxes.

Begin by talking about treasure, and the way pirates used to bury their treasure somewhere secret and hope to find it later with the aid of a map. Explain that you have found three such maps and need three intrepid explorers to find the hidden treasure. Send the first group off, and as they follow the map, talk about how we all seek treasure in our lives, and our treasure may be some smart clothes from the High Street, or a new set of golf clubs, or coming first in our exams, or getting a really dishy boy/girlfriend.

When they find the treasure, and the disappointment of not being able to unlock it, explain how the things we rush after are often not as satisfying as we thought they would be. Send the second group off, full of new hope. They will also be disappointed just as people in life sometimes get. Send the last lot off, and when they find the keys, explain that this is rather like us seeking God; it's a waste of time seeking all the other treasures, because we might as well go to the one who holds all the keys, not just to our two boxes but to a rich, fulfilling life, inner peace and everything we need.

Real freedom

Beforehand, prepare four official-looking files, labelled on the front in large letters, A, B, C and D. The information in the files reads something like this:

File A A is very bitter at being taken prisoner, and vows that he will get revenge as soon as possible. A spends his time cursing the waste of his life, and makes life as difficult as possible for everyone else in the prison.

File B B was very bitter at being taken prisoner, but then decided that he was only making his life worse, so asked God to use his imprisonment in some way for good. Over the year two other prisoners have met Jesus through talking to B, and their lives have been transformed. Many prisoners come to B when they feel down, because he makes them feel better.

File C C is a gifted runner with an excellent physique. He lets nothing at all interfere with his running. Due to this his marriage is breaking up and he never keeps friends because he is always letting them down. His parents are frail, but he never has time to visit them.

File D D is a gifted runner with an excellent physique. He has offered his running gift to God to use. Now that D is famous, he often gets asked about his life, and uses these opportunities to talk about how important Jesus is to him and what a difference being a Christian makes in his life. As a result, many of his followers have been introduced to the God of love.

First, have two people running up and down the aisle, labelled C and D, and two people sitting chained up, labelled A and B. Ask everyone which two people are in chains and which two are free.

Now explain that while that certainly looks obvious, we'll just check a few details out from their official files. Read out each in turn, asking/pointing out which ones are actually chained up, spiritually, and which are actually free. So our job is to live life to the full – however trapped or free we may physically feel.

Breaking the rules

Have a number of rules written out on large pieces of card. Choose rules appropriate to the experience of those present, such as:

Keep to the left in the corridors

No parking outside hospital entrance

Clear out pockets before dumping jeans for washing

Don't drink and drive

Hold up each in turn, asking people to work out what used to happen before the rule was made. Fill in the chart in each case, ticking as many columns as you like each time. Show how it is because we tend to be selfish / light-fingered / thoughtless that the rules need to be made. And in every case selfishness was to blame.

People were being:	Rule 1	Rule 2	Rule 3	Rule 4	Rule 5
SELFISH					
THOUGHTLESS					
LAZY					
LIGHT-FINGERED					
IRRESPONSIBLE					
FORGETFUL					

It makes God very sad to see us behaving like this because he designed us, not with self at the centre, but with love at the centre – love for God and love for one another. When we live like this, according to the maker's instructions, we feel free and happy, and the world is a better place in which to live.

Obey what is right

Ask for some volunteers and spread them around in the aisle. Explain that all you want is for them to do as they're told. Then give a series of instructions, such as right hand in the air, stand still, run on the spot, stretch arms out to the sides, touch your toes, touch your nose, and so on. Hardly give them time to think. Finish by telling them to go back to their seats and everyone can give them a round of applause for giving us such a stunning example of perfect obedience.

Point out that it's quite easy to be obedient when someone's shouting out instructions, and the things aren't too hard. But if you had told them to push everyone off their chairs, or give all their money to the vicar, would they have rushed to be obedient and carry out the instructions? Hopefully not! God forbid that we should be so keen to obey anyone that we fall in with any dangerous or wrong instruction. Teachers often come across children who have done something really stupid, and give the excuse that their friend told them to. Is that a good excuse? No, of course it isn't, because we have to think when we are asked to do anything, and refuse to do it if it seems selfish, dangerous or wrong. (It isn't just children, either – grown-ups will give as an excuse that everybody else does it, which is just as foolish an excuse, since everybody else could well be doing something dangerous or wrong.)

So where have we got to with obedience? That we are not meant to leave our brains and consciences behind. That means we are measuring every instruction up against the one we really trust to know what is right and good – underneath all the other obedient things we do there is a deep solid rock of obedience to God. That is what keeps us obedient wherever the instructions we are given are sensible and good, because measured up against the solid rock of our God we can see clearly that it's right to do what we're told here. In being obedient we are also being obedient to God.

And it's also what stops us obeying foolish, dangerous or wrong instructions which we might get from other people. Because when measured up against the solid rock of our God we can see clearly that to obey in those cases would make us disobedient to God.

Obedience to God is what matters more than anything, and Jesus showed us that.

Helpful criticism

Bring in a bike in unroadworthy condition and ask a couple of people who have recently passed their cycling proficiency test (or some other well-qualified person) to take a look at the bike and say what's good about it and what's in need of attention. As the items are mentioned, write them up on a chart in two columns.

Now we are in a much better position to put the bike right. We are quite happy to accept this as a sensible way of going on for a machine, but start getting very upset if the same sort of things are pointed out in us. Instead of welcoming fair criticism as a useful guide to help us put things right, most of us find criticism hurtful, and get upset about it. Yet we probably know the criticism is correct – we just didn't want anyone to notice! And we do want people to accept us and think well of us.

So let's try a double-ended approach; to think of criticism as a positive thing and welcome it as a means to put things right; and to make sure that whenever we need to criticise someone, we do it sensitively and lovingly, talking to them about it, not about them to someone else.

Don't just paper over the cracks

Beforehand, contact a local builder/decorator and ask if they would be willing to bring their tools and take part in a short interview during a service. (Well, why not – live dangerously!) Also bring with you a roll of wallpaper and a bag of paste. Start by introducing your guest, and say you've got problems with wallpaper peeling off and going mouldy, so would it be OK if you paste some of this new wallpaper over it?

As he goes through the stages of preparation and repair necessary ask him to show the specialist tools required, then ask him to tell you about the most difficult case he's ever tackled.

After this interview explain how we all have problems in our lives from time to time which are a direct result of sin. Like damp walls, sin needs sorting out thoroughly, not just covering over; if we try to cover over (as David did – 2 Samuel 11, 12), the sin and guilt don't go away, but make more problems. God is the only one able to sort our sin out by getting rid of it completely and making good afterwards, just as the experts do with walls.

First God S ... Shows us our sin,
then he I ... Invites us back to him;
but he N ... Never condemns us.

Blindness

You will need a blindfold, either a jacket with a hood or a length of bendy cardboard with tie-ups, and an optician's chart with the letters arranged like this:

Talk about the different kinds of blindness we meet in John 9. First there is the man who had been born blind. Ask someone to help you by being blindfolded. (If there is a blind person in your congregation you could ask them beforehand if they would mind being interviewed at this point.) Ask the blind/blindfolded person how it feels not to be able to see, which things they find particularly difficult and so on. If you are working with a blindfolded person, take the blindfold off and ask them how it feels to see again. Jesus enabled the blind man to see.

What about the Pharisees – the religious leaders? Were they blind or not? Ask for a volunteer and put on them the sight-restricting hood. What can they see and what can't they see? Explain how this can happen to any of us – we can be so rigid and concerned about a particular way of looking at things that we are effectively blind to anything outside our range of vision. Prejudice is like this hood; so is having a 'hobby horse about something' so that every conversation always comes round somehow to fishing, or the incompetence of a particular political party, or the trouble with young people today, or bad health.

Sometimes this tunnelled vision completely blocks people from seeing the good news of God's love. If they ask, Jesus can take those hoods off and enable them to enjoy full sight. But if they insist that they can see perfectly well already, then Jesus will be unable to help them and their narrowness is condemned.

Consequences

Begin by asking a couple of volunteers to run up and down, or jog on the spot and, as they do so, point out that if we choose to run fast like this there will be consequences. Stop the runners and demonstrate the way their breathing is much deeper and faster, and their pulse rate higher. They are probably warmer, too. All these things are natural consequences of the action they have been involved in.

If we choose to do something wise, like looking and listening carefully before we cross the road, we will have a far better chance of being safe. If you choose to do something foolish, like standing on your head when you haven't done so for 40 years, the likely consequence is that you will damage your neck. We make these decisions all the time and how we choose will actually change the shape of our characters.

If we choose the selfish, unkind, greedy, or cruel way we will become selfish, unkind, greedy or cruel people. If, on the other hand, we choose the friendly, encouraging, honest or loving way, we will become friendly, encouraging, honest or loving people. What we become will be a consequence of what we choose.

Temptation

You will need a tennis racket, a number of soft, sponge balls or balls of screwed up paper and a large cardboard carton.

First go through the story in 1 Samuel 26:1-12, bringing it to life. Ask people what David might have been thinking as he stood there over Saul. What might he have been tempted to do?

Temptations are bound to fly at us from all directions all through our lives. Ask someone to help you explain this by standing there as a group of people pelts them with balls. Sometimes the temptation is only slight (one ball) such as when you are tempted to kill your sister. You know deep down that though she irritates you, you wouldn't really want to do her any serious injury, so your fondness for her acts like a screen (they hold racquet up) and stops the temptation from getting any closer. (Throw ball so that the racquet screens the person.)

Sometimes the temptations fly at us so powerfully and urgently that even with the screen it is difficult to stop them getting to you. (Try this with lots of balls at once.)

What God provides for us is all-round protection. (Let the volunteer crawl into the large carton). If we make a habit of crawling into God's protection every day, then we will be better equipped to say 'NO!' to temptation. Don't try and fight off temptation on your own.

Be watchful

Beforehand, make these two traffic signs from card, or show them on a screen.

First ask some volunteers to play a game. One stands at the front holding a stop sign and the others go to the back. They have to get up to the front without being noticed. If the person at the front sees them moving s/he shows the stop sign and they must go and sit down. While the game is being played, keep distracting the person at the front and see what happens! If someone thinks they can be even more vigilant, try the game once more, now that everyone realises you are deliberately trying to distract their attention to prevent them being watchful.

Make the point that sin creeps up on us like this, little by little. It's all the day-to-day acts of meanness, selfishness, unkindness, dishonesty and so on that gradually make us comfortable behaving with cruelty and lack of love, until we're completely bitter, cynical and destructive people. Jesus warns us to be watchful, so we can stop (show the stop sign) bad habits before they get very far.

The trouble is that Satan doesn't like us being watchful and will try to distract us, often in ways which seem very nice and reasonable (as you were doing). So don't be deceived by that. Make a point of learning what is right (show the other sign) by spending time with Jesus in prayer every day, and don't let yourself be distracted from being watchful.

The judgement of God

Have ready three dustbin bags labelled SODOM, YOUR TOWN and SAM. You will also need a grid of some kind, such as a cooling tray. Inside each dustbin bag have some cut up shapes of blue and orange card, making sure that the orange shapes will fall through the holes in the grid and the blue ones won't. Put many more orange shapes than blue in the Sodom bag, about equal in your town's bag and more blue in Sam's bag. Finally you need a clear blue sign with GOOD written on it and an orange sign with EVIL on it.

First of all introduce everyone to the three bags. They can imagine Sam to be either male or female. He or she is just a fairly ordinary Christian with 2.4 children. Introduce your town with any appropriate remarks and introduce Sodom as another city – the one Abraham pleaded with God to save if a few good people could be found in it.

Can we see by looking at these bags how good or evil they are? No, we can't. But there's probably lots hidden from view which the light would show up to be good or evil. (Ask two volunteers to hold the good and evil signs so we know what we're looking for.)

It's when God's bright love shines that we see clearly what is good and what isn't. When we do that . . . (tip the Sodom bag up over the grid) God filters out the evil so that only the good survives.

The volunteers can comment on how much of the city of Sodom survived. Allow God's light to shine on the contents of the other bags in the same way.

The Church

God's family

Pick out two people of any age who belong to the same family and look alike or are wearing similar clothes. Tell everyone that they are from the same family. How can we tell? (Looks/mannerisms/clothes, etc.)

Now ask someone to pick out a scout/rainbow. How can we tell? (Uniform.) If I wore a scout uniform would I be a scout? What else is needed? I need to make my promise. As Christians we do that.

Could I be one of the Smith family? (No.) What if I made a promise? That's still not enough. For me to be one of the Smith family Mr and Mrs Smith would have to adopt me, and then I would be.

That's what God does. What is his son's name? (Jesus.) And God has adopted us as his sons and daughters, which makes us all brothers and sisters of one another and of Jesus, which makes us feel secure and comfortable and loved. That makes us want to behave lovingly to one another, because we're all 'family'. So we look after one another and forgive one another like our Father does.

Members of God's family

Begin by asking various groups of people to stand in quick succession: brothers, sisters, mothers, fathers, grandparents, grandchildren, aunts and uncles, nephews and nieces, cousins, sons and daughters. Some people will have stood up several times – that's fine. Everyone should have stood up at least once. (If the congregation is wary of standing up like this, I find it is less embarrassing for everyone to stand, and then the different categories sit.) So in our human families we may be several things at once – a dad may also be a cousin, a brother and a son, for instance.

We are also members of God's family. God is our Father – our parent – and, whatever our age, we are all his children. That means that everyone around us is a brother or sister. If you thought you didn't have any brothers and sisters, take a look around at some of your family!

What we need to do is to invite God into our homes – not as an occasional guest, but as a resident. We need to ask him to live with us. That way, our household will be filled with love, and we will find that we are able to treat one another with more love and care, and less irritability.

Chips off the old block

Beforehand, prepare two chunks of wood, which should be quite different from each other. From each cut a small chip. Also prepare some cards stuck on pea sticks and have a thick felt-tip pen at the ready to write in the signs.

First ask everyone what thing an ant might think of as huge. Then a cat. Then collect some ideas of what they themselves think of as huge. Remind everyone that all of these are contained in the mind of God and he is far greater than we can ever imagine. But let's have a go at imagining what God is like. Write the descriptions on the notices which people can hold up.

Now give out the two chips of wood and show everyone the blocks they came from. Ask a cluster of people round each chip to decide which block their chip came from. How can they tell? – By the way it feels; by its colour; by the grain, etc.

Jesus says that we are to behave in the same way God does – we are to be chips off the old block, and by looking at us and the way we behave, people should be able to recognise that we are Christians. So how will that mean we are to behave? Look again at the notices and they may be able to help us. If God is prepared to love everyone, whether they deserve it or not, then that's how we ought to be. If God is forgiving, we need to be as well. If God is trustworthy, so should we be to one another.

Look at the chips of wood again. If we're honest, we know we don't always behave like God. Jesus suggests that we recognise we are only chips and don't get carried away into thinking we're the block of wood. So long as we don't pretend we know all the answers he will be able to teach us through our lives to become more and more like him.

Chosen

Begin by talking about those times in games at school when the captains are choosing teams. Some people are always the ones left at the end which neither captain wants on their side. Others are fought over, because they're so skilled. Now, without mentioning what the team is for, ask a sporty-looking type from the congregation to choose a side, and have them all lined up holding a football, as in a team photograph.

Next tell them that they aren't actually a football team, but a washing and ironing team. Commiserate with the captain, asking if s/he's still happy with the people s/he chose, and giving the opportunity to change some members of his/her team if s/he wishes. (It will be interesting to see who is chosen now!) On a flip chart record how we go about choosing people for a job:

1. Know the people
2. Know the job

That way we can match up the needs with those who can best provide for the needs. And God does this all the time; because he knows us so well and knows people's needs so well, he can mix and match better than any of us. The trouble is, we often go rushing on to choose our own teams without really knowing what they will be needed to do.

If we look at the early church we find them taking time out to listen to God's ideas. They fasted – went without food – and spent a lot of time praying – spending time in God's company – and God chose two people to start the new mission who he knew would be best for the job. They were Paul and Barnabas. When you next have to make a choice or a decision, talk it over with God, and be prepared for him to put into your mind the name of someone you might never have even considered.

Jesus among us

Bring with you some items of clothing which alter the way you move when wearing them, such as a pair of flippers, a pair of very heavy boots, a pair of binoculars and a pair of very high-heeled shoes.

Invite volunteers to demonstrate that when they are wearing (or looking through) these, it changes the way they walk. The changed way of moving is all part of wearing them.

It isn't only clothes and footwear which change our way of going about; it's our thoughts and feelings as well. If we've just won a match, if (the person we love has just realised they love us as well, if the mortgage rate has gone down, or if we've just been fed and changed, then the whole day looks rosy and happy and we'll pass on our feel-good factor in the way we react to those we meet. On the other hand, if the cat's been sick on the new sofa, you've lost your spelling list and know you haven't learnt the words, if the no. 227 bus is half an hour late, or you're hungry and your bottom feels damp and sore, then those feelings will probably make you less friendly and forgiving, and far more grumpy!

When we look at the picture of life in the early Church in Acts 4:32-35, we're struck by how much love there seems to be in the community. Something is making these people happy to look after one another instead of fighting and arguing, and happy to share everything instead of looking after number one all the time. So what is making them like this? It must be something very good and very powerful!

It's all to do with them knowing something. They know that Jesus is alive and among them, so they are living in Jesus' company all the time. Jesus being there changes the way they live.

Now for a big question we all need to ask ourselves. Would anyone guess, just from looking at how we think and speak and behave, that we knew Jesus was living here among us?

He is, so it should show!

Filled with the Spirit

Protect the demonstration area with a groundsheet before starting the talk, just in case of spills. Have lots of buckets, jugs and mugs available, some empty and some with water in them.

Begin by explaining that all these represent people who go to church and are Christians. Sometimes, sadly, people may know all about Jesus, when he lived and what was and wasn't written about him, what everything in church is called and so on, but they are empty inside (tip the jug up). If anyone goes to them for a drink of God's love (try it), the person needing the drink will go away thirsty – they won't be able to get refreshed or comforted or healed or loved because the person they thought could help them is all dried up inside.

Let's try another Christian. (Try another container.) That's much better – this Christian is full of the loving Spirit of God so the thirsty person will come into close contact with God's love through them.

Look at all the different shapes of containers. We don't have to be a special shape of Christian to qualify. We may be simple or dramatic (choose containers to emphasise this), tall or short, Evangelical or Catholic. God is delighted to pour his Spirit into all of these, but one thing is necessary for all of us: we need to go to the source to be filled. We need to tell God that we want him to fill us with his living Spirit, and when he starts to, we need to keep ourselves open so that he can. He may fill us full in a rush, or he may gently fill us bit by bit; however he chooses to do it will be the very best way for us.

Sharing the workload

Beforehand, arrange for two piles of extremely bulky, cumbersome items to be put at the front of the church.

Explain that you would like these two sets of equipment / junk moved down to the back of the church, out of the way. Invite three or four people to work on one lot, and one person on the other. Invite everyone else to watch what happens. It should become apparent that the group found it both easier and quicker than the person on his/her own, who is probably left struggling and tired at the end of the operation. Suggest that many of us have felt like that struggling, weary person, when everything feels too much to cope with, and yet we know the job has to be done.

That's how Moses felt (Exodus 18:13-26), sorting out everybody's problems, and teaching them God's ways. The job had just become too big for one person to cope with, and that's why Jethro sensibly suggested the load sharing by other wise, trustworthy people.

We need to look out for anyone struggling on their own in ministries within our church, and offer to help. (If there are any particular needs, why not mention them here.) It doesn't make God happy to see a few of his children burning themselves out unnecessarily when there are others to share the load. Load sharing doesn't just get things done quicker; it builds up the love and fellowship of the church as people work together, encourages a deepening of faith and joy in believing, and guards against the onset of resentment and bitterness which are so often born of overwork.

Together with Christ

Have ready some pieces of card with these diagrams on them:

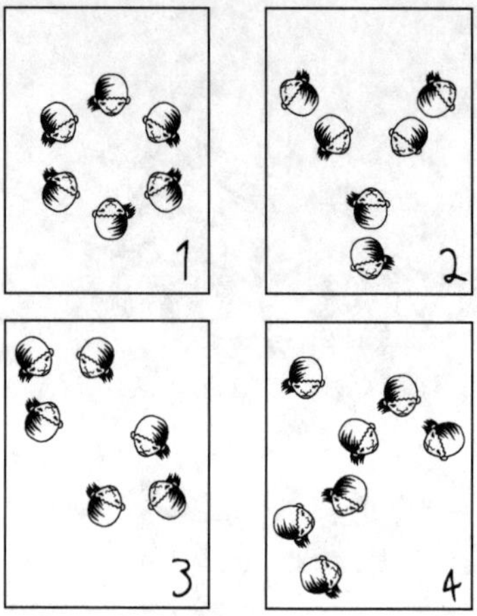

Explain that we often spend time looking at what is supposed to happen in life. Today we are going to look at what actually happens, more often than not. Ask six volunteers to make up the first diagram. Here are all these nice friends, and before long they start getting cross with one another and having arguments and upsetting one another. (Ask them each to find an adversary from within the group.)

Give one of each couple a red team band to wear, and give the others blue bands. Explain that all this blue-banded lot get together and feel at one because they have a common enemy – all those other horrors with red bands. (They move into diagram two.) Then the isolated people with red bands find they have grievances in common and move together. (Form diagram three.) Within their own groups they can feel really acceptable by being different from and superior to the other group – and can we think of some real-life examples of this? (Such things as racial prejudice, gangs, exclusive sects and tribes.)

What happens when a strong outsider arrives on the scene, trying to make peace? (Ask one to join in.) What often happens is that now the two groups join up so as to fight the common enemy. (Move into diagram four.) They have become united and put aside their differences, emphasising now what they have in common against the new enemy – they all have bands and she doesn't. Can we think of some real-life examples of this?

(A coalition government during war, or civil rights campaigns.) It's a very human way to behave, and it means a lot of people spend their lives fighting.

Jesus can help. He draws us all together so that no one is left out, and we all have a common enemy which is evil. At our baptism we are asked, 'Do you renounce evil?' and we reply, 'We renounce evil!' (Try this now.) Together in Christ's love and power, we are made one.

Jesus' family

Whether we live on our own or with others, most of us have family; we may not see them that often, or we may see them every day. Some of them may no longer be alive, but they are still our family. Mothers and fathers, stepmothers and stepfathers, parents-in-law and children-in-law, sons and daughters, grandchildren and grandparents, aunts and uncles, brothers, sisters and cousins, are all family. We share the same genes (and sometimes the same jeans).

In every family there is something called a family resemblance – a family likeness. (Some family members may be willing to demonstrate this likeness.) The DNA within our families shows up right across the generations; in my family there's the Morris nose, the Rackett musicality, and the Orme stubborn determination, for instance!

In Mark 3:31-35, Jesus says something rather amazing. He's sitting teaching, surrounded by a closely packed circle of faces, people from all kinds of different families and backgrounds, with all kinds of different looks and personalities. They are there because they sense that in Jesus they can get closer to the true, living God than they've ever been before. They are so keen that they are hanging on every word Jesus speaks, listening to him intently.

And as he looks around at them sitting there, and sees in their eyes their love of God, Jesus happily counts all of them – and everyone else who does the will of God – as members of his close family. He is saying that any of us, however ordinary or damaged, whatever natural family we belong to, or are separated from, are close members of Jesus' family! So you can think of yourself as closely related to Jesus. And that makes all of us in the Church part of the same family, distinguished by the family likeness of doing God's will – living the loving way.

Witnesses

With a couple of people warned beforehand, stage a crime, such as a handbag snatch, in front of everyone's eyes. Then accuse an innocent person of committing the crime. S/he appeals for witnesses. Interview a couple of witnesses and let everyone vote on the strength of their eyewitness accounts as to the person's innocence. (Hopefully the person should be proved innocent – if s/he isn't, I suggest you go on quickly to the next hymn, or trade your congregation in for a different model!)

Point out how important witnesses are; if they have seen something and don't speak out about it, they are partly to blame for a miscarriage of justice. If we have seen what a difference Jesus makes in our lives and know that he really is alive, then we are called to be witnesses to that, so that all those in our lost and weary world may find the joy of his love for themselves. If we don't, how are they to know?

So, how do we witness?

a) By our lives.

b) By our words.

Going back to the crime that was committed here this morning, could those a long way off be effective witnesses? No. In this case that was out of their control, but being Christ's witnesses, the closer we get to Jesus, and the more time we spend with him, the more effective witnesses we shall be.

Telling others

Arrange beforehand for someone to be wearing their coat or sweater inside out, and for someone's bag to be mislaid.

Start by saying you need a volunteer, and choose the person with their clothing on inside out. Pretend you are rather embarrassed at having to tell them something, and then tell them about their clothing and help them put things right. Ask everyone if they think you should have mentioned it, or whether you should have kept quiet. If your sound system makes it possible, allow a few people to put their points of view.

Explain that if we can see something that is really wrong, and don't tell the person lovingly about it, they won't be able to put things right. And if we're on the receiving end, we might wish we did know where we are going wrong, or hurting someone, because then we are in a position to do something about it.

The prophets were shown what God wanted them to say to the people, and the ones who listened were the ones who saw God's word as an opportunity for growth, rather than as a destructive threat.

Now ask if anyone has mislaid their bag this morning. Ask if anyone knows anything about this. No one does. Point out that if we are in possession of good news and don't let on, then this person will stay worried and upset. Now the person who knows where the bag is stands up and tells the good news, and the bag is found. (A round of applause if you're that kind of congregation; polite smiles if you're not.)

There are lots of people in our world who are lost, and confused and scared inside or lonely because they haven't yet met anyone who introduced them to the living Jesus. And if you meet them, and don't share your good news with them, they will have to go on being miserable. Ask people to turn to the person next to them, and in twos and threes tell one another why they love God already, or why they are interested in finding out more about him. After a minute or two, ask if any four people would be brave enough to stand up on their own and say why they love God. Point out how difficult this is to do in the middle of sympathetic listeners, let alone with a hostile audience. We need to remember that being a witnessing community is not easy, and we need to keep close to God the whole time, supporting one another with prayer.

Worship and life

Beforehand, you will need to collect six cartons of a similar size and cover them back and front with plain paper.

Arrange the boxes as shown. Draw a picture of three people on one side and write on the other: WE WORSHIP GOD. Write the same words on a long strip of paper which everyone will be able to see.

First of all remind everyone of how close Christmas is getting, and do a check on who has already made the pudding/got presents/wrapped them up/sent cards, etc. So preparations are well under way. But we need to prepare our lives as well, and how is that going?

Arrange the boxes in the right shape but totally out of order and explain that it is a picture of the lives of Christians. Proudly drape a long strip of paper over the boxes and ask everyone if all is well as they look rather puzzled. When someone says the boxes are out of order, say something like, 'Well, these words say they worship God so they must be right, mustn't they?'

What the prophets did was challenge the people who said they worshipped God, but who lived as if they hardly gave him a thought. It happens today as well – we can get used to saying the words, but do our lives match up?

Ask a couple of volunteers to sort the words and pictures out so that they do match up with what they are saying. The whole thing can be viewed from both sides – when the words are really true, the people themselves are sorted out as well. And that's how it is with us – if we say we worship God, then we must sort our lives out so that they match up with what we are saying and, as we do so, we shall become more integrated, fulfilled people.

Welcome?

Beforehand, arrange with two people from another church to come to your church as strangers today, asking one to dress in a way which fits in well with the people in your congregation, and the other in a way which might be difficult for the congregation to accept. This needs some careful thought! Ask them to come into church separately, and make it clear to the sidespeople that they aren't used to coming here.

At the beginning of the talk have a box with a closed lid. Is it open or closed? Now open it a little. Is it open or closed now? Then open it up fully. Is it open or closed? We are like this with other people and with God. With some people we are very open, with others we are a little open, and with others, we shut up tight. God's teaching today advises us to be wide open to God, so that we are able to be open and welcoming to others.

Now invite the two 'strangers' to the front, and explain the awful truth that you invited them specially to help us look at our own hospitality. Ask them how it felt to be coming in as strangers, and what would need to happen (or happened) to put them at their ease. This needs to be done with sensitivity, humour, and without any sense of accusation, of course. Point out how it is natural for us to find some people easier to get on with than others, and that as we realise God's love for us more and more, we shall be more and more able to reach out to others, even those who would not naturally be our friends.

Family and neighbours

Family

If you have stained glass windows, direct people to look at these during the talk. If not, bring a picture or poster which is full of contrasting colours, or have such a picture or photograph projected on to a screen.

Draw everyone's attention to the different colours that are used, asking them to pick out their favourites, to pick out some of the darks and some of the lights. Perhaps there are also different textures involved.

Explain that family life is rather like this – a whole picture made up of bright and dark colours, of happy and sad times, angry and contented times, worrying and relaxed times. Ask for examples of these from everyone, so that our own colourful picture starts to take shape.

It isn't just us on our own who are making these family works of art – it's us and God together, and we go on making them all through our lives. Whenever there is a whole lot of dark, sad colour, God will brighten it for us with the rich, warm colours of his comforting love.

God and our families

On a large sheet of paper have two columns, headed like this:

Family life

The nice things	**The nasty things**

Give people a minute to talk in pairs about the nice things before collecting ideas on the chart, then do the same with the nasty things. Reassure people that all families have both, and that helps us learn to forgive, because we get lots of practice.

Point out that God used the jealousy and double dealing in Jacob's family to bring good in the end (Genesis 45). Joseph was able to help the family in a crisis and by bringing them to Egypt he made it possible for the nation of Israel to form in Goshen. Even the things which threaten to split a family apart can be used for good if we let God in to work. Family life is to do with helping one another. Do we make life easier for others in our home, or harder? Do we pull our weight as part of the team, or expect someone else to do everything for us? Talk it over with God and listen to what he puts into your mind over the next few days.

Today could be the first day of you changing things and helping to make your home a happier place.

The cost of love

You will need a bucket, a ball of string, two full bags from the local supermarket, a pair of children's trainers, a cheque book and credit card.

Talk about what things cost, asking the prices of such things as a bottle of lemonade, a sliced loaf, a five-litre pot of emulsion, etc. Point out how the cost is known by those who have wanted or needed these things; our want or need pushes us to find out the cost so that we can work out whether we can afford it or not.

What about the cost of bringing up a child for a year? Let's check that out. It's something like 52 trips to Safeways (dump the shopping bags down) a couple of pairs of trainers, a chequebook full of club subscriptions, school uniform, birthday presents and a holiday, and a credit card bill of petrol for the chauffeur service. But that's not all – it also costs an enormous length of patience (unravel the string up the whole length of the aisle) and 365 buckets of love, a fresh bucket for every day of the year.

If we look around, we'll find quite a few parents who are more than happy to pay that cost for the privilege of a year's worth of son or daughter! That's how God feels about us – he is glad to pay what it costs to set us free from our guilt and sin and worry and fear, even though the cost is incredibly high – rejection and ridicule, pain and death by crucifixion. That's a huge number of buckets of love.

Neighbours

Begin by playing the theme tune of *Neighbours,* if you can stand it! Point out how the words are all about good neighbours becoming good friends – all very noble stuff – and yet most episodes are largely taken up with the feuds and grumps of those living around the Ramsay Street area. Quarrels, we suppose, are far more lifelike, and make better viewing.

Talk everyone through the Ahab and Jezebel 'bad neighbours' plot (1 Kings 21:1-24), where Naboth gets a very raw deal through the king's sulks and the queen's efficient cruelty. How do we react when people won't give us what we want? Learning to accept that we can't have things we want is often a hard, though very valuable lesson to learn. The more we work at accepting other people – whatever they look, sound or smell like – the less we shall find ourselves being driven crazy by them. We may not agree with what they do, but we won't be holding grudges, nurturing resentment or waging guerrilla warfare.

The law of love

Have a large sign prepared which says:

LOVE GOD
LOVE YOUR NEIGHBOUR
AS YOURSELF

and have ready a number of smaller pieces of card and a marker pen.

Ask two people to hold the sign so everyone can read it and invite everyone to do just this. Explain how this truth was shown to Moses, and through him to all the people of Israel. God wants this close relationship of love with his people, and that spills over into the way we treat one another.

Unfortunately, people being people, gradually lots of other details about the basic law of love crept in, partly to explain it in practical ways. Ask people to suggest some practical details arising from the basic rule, and write each one on another piece of card, inviting someone to hold it up, until the original message is hardly visible through all the fussy details. (Details might be such things as:

- go to worship twice a week
- say your prayers at least twice a week
- don't do any work at all on Sundays.)

Explain that some of the teachers of the law in Jesus' time had got over-enthusiastic with their detailed rules, and some of them had lost sight (as we have) of the real meaning of God's law of love. So what Jesus did was to clear away all these extra bits (do so) and reveal the law again in all its beauty. It is a beautiful thing to live lovingly – responding to God's love for you, and passing on that love to others.

Sharing burdens

Beforehand, ask someone to walk up the centre of the building when the talk begins, carrying a fully packed backpack, as if they are going camping.

Begin by saying we are going to be thinking about heavy loads, and when the camper arrives, interview them about the best way to pack things so that you don't put your back out before you start. Unpack some of the items so that everyone can see the weight-saving that goes on and the care that is taken in making the load as easy as possible. But it's still pretty heavy!

In our lives we are probably all carrying a load of some kind. A load is something which makes you weighed down, and we may feel weighed down from our concern about a close friend or relative who is suffering or is in with the wrong crowd. Or the pressure of work demands may weigh us down, or the strain of living in an unhappy environment, or the fear of a bully at school. All these things can feel like heavy burdens. For many in the world the burden is not having enough to eat, not being able to feed your children, not having your home any more, or not being able to get treatment for a loved one who is very ill. Some of these weights can be made a little easier by ourselves, but for most of them we need to share the weight with others, who can help take the strain. To do that, two things are needed:

1. For us to be willing to share another person's load.
   (Let a volunteer come and pick up an empty backpack.)
2. For us to be willing to let others help us.
   (The camper agrees to be helped, and together they share the load.)

Living together

Ask for two volunteers of about the same height (or several pairs of volunteers) and tie the ankles of each pair together. They can practise walking three-legged around the church. As they do so, point out how difficult it is until you get the hang of walking in step with one another. This is one of the most important lessons we can learn in life.

We are all given other people to live with. People in our families like brothers and sisters, mums, dads, grandparents, aunts, uncles and cousins. Is it easy, just because we are related? No! Sometimes it's very good fun, like when we're all getting on together and making one another laugh, and listening to what the others are saying, and the others understanding when you come home fed up.

At other times it's very hard living with those close to us. Like when everyone wants something different and no one wants to do the washing-up, and so on. That's a bit like when we get in a tangle of feet in the three-legged race and trip one another up. When we start to think it would be a lot easier to live on our own without other people around.

What St Paul suggests is that we need to live in step with one another, learning to do things like forgiving one another, being patient, letting someone else have the best sometimes, co-operating instead of getting at each other's throats all the time (see Colossians 3:12-17). That's the Christian way. That's Jesus' way. It may also mean comforting one another, sharing one another's suffering. It's really learning to love in the way Jesus talked about love.

When we live like this, we and the people we are joined up with, in our families and at school and at work, won't need to keep tripping one another up. We'll be able to live more supportively, enjoying one another as God meant us to.

Faith

Seeing the invisible

You will need a hairdryer or a fan, or a lit candle to blow out.

Start with a riddle. You're thinking of something which is all around us, pressing against our faces and bodies at 15 pounds per square inch. It goes in and out of us all the time we're alive, and there's lots of it right in front of our eyes. What is it? (Air.) But we can't see it, so how do we know it's there?

Put on the hairdryer or fan, or ask someone to blow the candle out. When air moves, we can see what it does. When we try to hold our breath we realise how much our bodies need air to live.

God is here as well, and we can't see him. No one has ever seen God while they are alive on earth. So how can God tell us what he is like, when we can't see him?

There are ways we can see what God is like by what he does and by what he creates. If we look at the world we can see that God must be generous, imaginative, careful, clever, organised, hopeful and happy to let us work with him.

But God had an even better idea. If he could walk among humans as a human, then all the humans who lived at the time or at any time afterwards would be able to see exactly how God behaves. We could see it in our own human language. The language of doing, thinking, feeling and speaking.

In John 1:1-18 Jesus is talked about as being the Word, or the Message of God. When we look at how Jesus lived and died, we are looking straight at God, even though we can't see God with our eyes.

And what do we see? John describes Jesus as being 'full of grace and truth'. Have this written up on a sheet. Around it you can add other people's ideas. Head the page 'Jesus is' and display it for the rest of the service.

Growing in faith

Beforehand, ask a family to help you by providing a couple of clothing items which are now too small for their child to wear. Or you could borrow a cub/brownie sweater which once you would have been able to get into. Also find a sprouting acorn, or a similar example of life bursting out of confines.

Begin by talking about the way we grow out of our clothes. Sometimes we like a sweater or jacket so much that we want to go on wearing it even when it's a bit short or tight, but eventually we realise that we just can't get into it any more, and we'll have to hand it down to someone younger or smaller. As you talk about this, use the children and their skimpy clothes to illustrate how silly it looks and how uncomfortable it feels to wear something which is much too small for us, and then try the same garment on someone it fits to see the difference.

Remind everyone that we are spiritual as well as physical, and we can grow out of things spiritually as well. Some of the early Christians thought that it wasn't right for non-Jewish people to be allowed to join the Church. In Acts 11:1-18 Peter realised that was like wearing a sweater which was too small, and God's ideas were much bigger than they had thought. He wanted everyone to be part of his love, with no one left out. So the early church very sensibly took off that outgrown idea.

When we are very young, we are taught to pray prayers we can understand. That's wonderful. But if we are still praying like a 3 year-old when we are 13 or 23, or 53, we are wearing skimpy spiritual clothes that we have really outgrown. Unless we realise that, and take them off, and find ways of praying that fit, we won't be able to move forward where God wants us to go.

Take a look at the acorn. Acorns are lovely to hold and play with, just as they are. But the oak tree can't become its huge, leafy self unless it breaks out of the acorn, and leaves that behind.

Jesus gives us all a rule, or command. We are to love one another. As soon as we start this kind of responsible, caring love for one another, we are bound to start growing. Sometimes the growing hurts. Sometimes the growing feels exciting. Sometimes the growing is hard work. And always the growing will be breaking out of where we were before. This means that, like children growing taller year by year, we will not be able to keep wearing the same old spiritual clothes. God won't let us get set in our ways because he goes on having exciting plans for us right through our lives, no matter how old we get.

Seeing and believing

Beforehand, place a CD in your pocket. Begin by telling everyone that you have got an orchestra in your pocket and asking them if they believe you. Then show them the CD. Now they have seen with their eyes they know exactly what was in your pocket. And now that they understand what it is, they can see that you were right – you did have an orchestra in your pocket, but not in the way they expected!

Jesus had told his friends that he would have to suffer and die before rising to new life, and they hadn't understood what he meant. Even when Jesus was dying, nailed to the cross, they didn't realise that this had to happen if we were to be saved from sin and death. Instead they felt miserable and let down and lost and confused. They didn't believe because they hadn't seen for themselves. (Put the CD back in your pocket.)

Then, on the first Easter evening, Jesus was suddenly there with them. He was alive, talking with them and they were so excited and overjoyed to have him there again. Now that they had seen him they knew it was true that he was alive (see John 20:19-29). (As you say this bring out the CD from your pocket again, but don't refer to it. It will simply help them make connections.)

But it was also different from what they might have thought. Jesus wasn't exactly the same as before. With this new life he was able to be there without having unlocked the doors. He could appear and disappear. But he was a real person, not a ghost. He didn't make the disciples feel scared; he filled them with peace and happiness.

At last they began to understand what he had meant when he had talked to them about dying and rising again. They began to understand that God's love had to go right through death, loving and forgiving the whole way, so as to win the battle against evil. When Jesus came through death and out into the light of new life, he was like a butterfly coming out of its chrysalis – the same but completely different, free and beautiful.

Thomas and the others needed to see Jesus with their eyes for quite a few times after the Resurrection. They now had to learn that he was always there with them, even if they couldn't see him.

Don't worry!

Beforehand, prepare some large speech bubbles from thin card, with the typical worries of those in the congregation written clearly on them. Here are some suggestions:

- My hair's going grey/thin on top!
- What can I wear?
- Weetabix or cocopops or toast?
- Suppose they don't like me?
- Leather or denim – and how much of it?
- I'm the wrong shape!

Ask some volunteers to hold these worries up high. They're the kind of things we all waste our time and energy worrying about. Jesus was sad to see people worrying their lives away, and he wanted them to be free of this constant worrying. Point out that the volunteers will start to get aching arms if they have to go on holding the worries up for too long.

Matthew tells us that Jesus says to us, 'Put all those worries down – they're heavy to carry and are making your arms ache.' (See Matthew 6:25-34) Let the volunteers put the worries down, and talk about what a relief it is to have our worries sorted out.

Jesus wants us to know that although life is bound to be full of difficult and uncomfortable times as well as easy and happy times, we don't need to worry about it as well as live through it! That makes it twice as bad for us. The way to be free of worry is not to be massively rich or refuse to grow up, or bury your head in the sand and pretend not to see the problems. The way to be free of worrying yourself sick is to trust that your Parent God loves you, likes you, and is well able to help you cope with everything you'll face in your life.

Jesus suggests we live one day at a time, instead of worrying about things that might never happen, or which are bound to happen, and God will bring us safely through it all to heaven, where we will be safe with God for ever.

Learning to trust

Ask for one volunteer who is brave and one who is more scared and timid. Tell the timid one that you are asking them to fall backwards. You promise them they won't come to any harm (but you don't say you will catch them). Suggest that they watch the brave volunteer to try it first, so they can see what happens. Now ask the brave volunteer to fall backwards, and make sure you catch them, or arrange to have someone strong to catch them.

Now ask if the timid person is able to try it, now that they have seen that it is safe. If they are, let them try it, making certain they are safely caught!

Sometimes it is very hard to know whether we can trust something or not unless we have seen it in action. Perhaps we have bought a CD player, or a jigsaw puzzle at a boot sale or a jumble sale, and it looks fine, and we are assured that it's in good working order. But when we get home we find the CD player skips, and the jigsaw puzzle has two or three pieces missing.

It's all very disappointing to be let down like that. And the longer we live, and the more we are let down by things or by people, the more disappointed we get, and the more determined we are not to trust anyone or anything in case we are let down again. Thomas was a bit like that. He had probably been badly let down by people during his life. Like lots of us, it made him scared to trust good news. We and Thomas would love good news to be true, but we'd rather not trust it at all than trust it and risk being let down.

Now Jesus himself knows that he is alive, and will stay alive for ever. He knows it would be quite safe for us to believe this, because he knows it's true! He hopes very much that we will be able to believe, because he knows it will make such a wonderful difference to our lives – we'll be able to live in a new kind of freedom, and become more and more our real selves.

So what does he do about it? In John 20:19-29 we hear how Jesus came into the room, joining his friends as they were praying, so that they knew he was there. And Jesus still does that, nearly two thousand years later. He is here now, with us, his friends. Whenever we gather in Jesus' name, he joins us. When we live on the lookout for him, we'll find we start noticing him more and more. We won't see him with our eyes, but we'll feel his love and peace, and suddenly know he is there.

Go for it!

Beforehand collect some 'special offers' from your junk mail during the week and from local shops. Also make one sign that says, 'Not today, thanks!' and another that says, 'Yes, I'll go for it!' Ask everyone (or just the children) to shout out the words on the signs whenever you show them.

Start by talking about the special offers in your collection, referring to those which people of different ages in the congregation might find interesting, amusing and completely ridiculous. Ask a volunteer to display the general view of people about various offers by holding up the appropriate sign. Point out that in all these special offers we are free to choose whether to take advantage of the offer or not, and if it's something we really want and like we're likely to say, 'Yes, I'll go for it!' If we don't think we need the item on offer then we don't think it's worth having and we're more likely to say, 'Not today, thanks!'

Jesus' special offer to us is extremely good value. He offers to make himself at home in our lives and set us free from all the things that imprison us, so that we can really live to the full, not just now, but after death as well. For ever, in fact. How much does it cost? Nothing. Or rather, everything, but Jesus has already paid the complete cost for us.

As it's such a good offer you'd think that everyone would rush to take him up on it. (Display the 'Yes, I'll go for it!' sign.) But Luke 13:34 tells us that there have always been lots of people who have refused the offer and turned it down. (Display the 'Not today, thanks!' sign.) In this verse we see Jesus really sad. What has made him so sad is that he has been longing to give people the love he knows they need and yet they won't let him give them this free gift which could make their whole lives rich.

Perhaps we don't think we need God's love and help. Perhaps we are afraid to accept because it seems just too good to be true. Perhaps we think it can't be possible because we don't think we're worth something as good as this. Whatever the reasons, lots of us humans end up saying 'Not today, thanks!' to the best special offer ever. That means losing out on all the good things God is hoping to give us during our lives on earth and our lives in heaven. Things like joy and peace of mind, contentment and fulfilment, a sense of really being alive and living life the best way there is.

Abram was a 'Yes, I'll go for it!' person. He took God up on his offer and believed God would put his action where his mouth was. As a result his life was greatly blessed. And God did keep his promise to make Abram's descendants as many as the uncountable stars in the sky.

God will never force us to say 'Yes, I'll go for it!' when we really want to say 'Not today, thanks!' But before anyone says 'Not today, thanks!' to God's special offer of his freely given love, they would be wise to think it over very carefully. It's such a fantastic offer that the only wise thing to say is, 'Yes, I'll go for it!'

Fashion or faith?

Beforehand gather a selection of brand-name items relevant to each age group in the congregation.

Begin by displaying each item and drawing attention to the brand name to impress people. Talk about how we are sometimes made to feel we have to have a particular thing in order to be thought normal or worth anything. Sometimes we are teased if we haven't got them. Sometimes we go out shopping to cheer ourselves up, thinking that having more will make us happy. Sometimes we spend money we can't afford to keep up with our friends or neighbours.

Put all the items into a carton labelled 'Very Important' and close the lid. Explain that Jesus turns our ideas of what is important upside down. As you say this, turn the carton upside down. Jesus told people that trust in what you can buy and possess is not the good thing the advertisements say it is, and these things don't give us long-term happiness at all (see Luke 12:15-34).

So what does he offer instead?

Jesus says that we will be much happier if we trust in God rather than in things people say about us, and things people make and sell. Getting stuck in the 'wanting something else' mode or the 'everybody else does it' mode just ends up making us dissatisfied and greedy and selfish, which doesn't bring happiness to us or those we live with. But if we put our trust in God, all the riches of the kingdom of God will be ours. We'll enjoy the lovely and surprising ways God provides for our needs. We'll be able to see what is good and right, and want to work enthusiastically again instead of just going through the motions. We won't be frantically running to keep up with the latest fashion. We won't be so anxious about material things.

Jesus doesn't say we'll have lots of comforts or fame or money if we live like this. In fact he says we will run into insults and people will think we're crazy, and they will laugh at us and make life difficult for us. We can't say we haven't been warned!

But the rewards far outweigh the disadvantages. Putting our trust in God will enable us to live as free, contented and generous-hearted people – the kind of people we would, deep down, probably prefer to be.

Real faith

Explain that we are going to find out what faith is by discovering what it isn't. To make a point, have the word 'FAITH' drawn really faintly on a large sheet of paper.

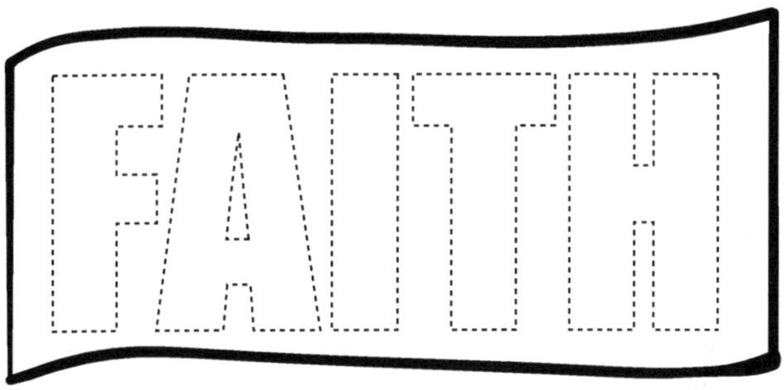

As each thing that isn't faith is talked about, some of the outside is coloured in, until the whole word appears in white, through the background being filled in.

Suppose you jumped out of an aeroplane, feeling sure that God would stop you getting killed; or you were sure that when you got up in the morning, God would have arranged for all the washing-up to be done; is that real faith? No – it's certainly odd, though. Faith in God isn't magic.

What about having faith that God will give us everything we ask, so we ask him for a bike or a new car. When we don't get it we can safely say that God doesn't exist. Is that real faith? No, all that proves is that God isn't a slot machine, which we knew already.

Or what about faith being a kind of wishful thinking. God doesn't really exist, but if we want to pretend he does and that makes us feel better, then we can, so long as we don't take it too seriously. Lots of people think like this. They think of us with a sort of pity, and wonder when we'll grow up. So is faith in God wishful thinking? No, faith would only be a 'let's pretend' game if God didn't exist.

Faith in God means recognising the truth that God is real, alive and active. When we have faith in him we are prepared to trust him to lead us, advise us, heal us and even use us so as to let more people have the fulfilment they long for.

Ask everyone to shut their eyes. Now they can't see the church around them. But it doesn't mean it isn't there. (Open eyes to check!) Sometimes we can feel God's presence very strongly, and that's exciting. Sometimes we can't feel anything but that doesn't mean God has disappeared – it just means we aren't aware of him at the moment. The more we listen and watch for signs of his presence, the more we will notice them. And the tragedy is that those signs are staring people in the face sometimes, and because they are so sure God doesn't really exist, they do not see him reaching longingly out to their misery, in love.

The wisdom of faithfulness

Today is a good opportunity to celebrate the elderly faithful and build relationships between young and old. Beforehand arrange for an elderly man and woman to sit at the front with a microphone to answer a few questions put to them by the children about what life was like when they were children. Gather the children round their feet and introduce the elderly people. Since they have been alive a long time they have picked up lots of wisdom. They have lived through things the younger ones here have heard about in history. Invite the children to find out what it was like being a child 70 or more years ago – they can ask about clothes, toys, school, church or food, for instance. After a few questions thank the volunteers and have the children escort them back to their seats.

When Jesus was a baby, Joseph and Mary brought him into the temple (see Luke 2:22-38). All Jewish families did this when their first son was born. They came to give a present, or offer a sacrifice to God and dedicate the child. We've had two wise, elderly people answering questions today. And when Mary, Joseph and Jesus came into the temple there were two wise elderly people there. Their names were Simeon and Anna. They had both loved God all their life, and if any of us do that, we will end up wise and lovable in our old age. You can't love God all your life and end up crabby and narrow-minded.

Jesus didn't have a big label tied round his swaddling clothes saying 'I am the Messiah'. Joseph and Mary didn't wave flags or shout to everyone, 'Look! This is the baby you've all been waiting for!' From the outside he looked just like any other baby, and Mary and Joseph looked just like an ordinary, fairly poor set of parents, rather dusty after the journey.

So how did Simeon and Anna know that this baby was the one they were waiting for?

Simeon had been told that he would see the promised Messiah in person before he died. He had been listening to God all his life, and because he was used to listening to God, he was able to recognise that this particular baby was the Messiah, God's chosen one.

When we spend a lot of time with another person we get to know how they think, and we understand them better and better. If we spend time with God every day, starting from today, and carry on doing that right into our old age, we will get to know him better and better, and it won't be long before we are able to hear what he speaks into our hearts.

It is astounding that the powerful creator of this universe is happy to communicate with individuals like this, but that's God for you. He's hoping there will be some wise and faithful elderly Christians in the future – twenty, thirty, forty, fifty, sixty, seventy or eighty years from now. There could be. It could be us.

Parables

Seeds and soil

You will need a seed tray filled with seed compost, some large-sized seeds, a dibber (to poke holes for the seeds) and a cloth bag of pearl barley. You will also need to arrange for a broom to sweep up the scattered barley after the talk. Lay down in the aisle one large piece of paper to represent a rocky patch, and a few footprints to represent a stony path.

You might like to play a snatch of *In an English Country Garden* at the beginning, as you set out the seed tray and compost on a table and invite a couple of keen gardeners in the congregation to demonstrate planting. As the gardeners work, talk with them about why the seed planted like this is more likely to be successful than if we just shake the seeds outside.

In Matthew 13:1-9 Jesus told a parable which was all about seeds being sown, and the best growing conditions. Of course, it wasn't just about seeds being planted and growing. Parables are stories with secrets inside, and the secret of this story is that it was really all about us, and how we respond to God's word when we hear it. This is how it works.

Where Jesus lived, it was very rocky, and the farmers had fields with bare rock showing here and there (put down the paper), and stony roads that went right through the middle (put down the footprints). They ploughed the earth in long furrows, like we did here in the seed tray, only much bigger of course, and then the person sowing the seed walked up and down the furrows sowing the seed like this. (Demonstrate with your bag of pearl barley, scattering the seed to left and right.) The problem is that not all the seed goes in the nice soil you have prepared. When God's word is spoken, we are not always ready to accept it. Let's look at where some of those seeds have landed.

Invite a volunteer to look at the stony path and stand over any seeds they find there. Sometimes we read or hear God's teaching and we're more like a stony path than good soil. It just goes in one ear and out of the other, and we hardly notice what we've heard. We might sit here for the readings and our thoughts fly in, like birds, and take away God's message so we don't even remember what was said.

What about the rocky ground? (Send a volunteer there.) Sometimes we hear God's message and get really keen, and take on far too much far too early, so, like plants growing up on rocky soil, we haven't got good roots. We burn ourselves out and drop away.

What about the soil next to the rock? (Send a volunteer there.) Lots of weeds grow here, so there's a lot of competition for the seeds. Sometimes we hear God's message, but there are so many other things going on in our lives, which we consider important, that the really important message of God gets choked and crowded out.

But all the rest is in good soil. We are like good soil when we listen to God's teaching carefully, think about it and what it means, and then live with it. That way we shall certainly grow and produce a good harvest. Let's check this week that we are taking good notice of God's words to us, and giving him proper space and time, so that we grow in his love.

Lost sheep

Gather a mixed group of 'sheep', and appoint a shepherd who is given a crook. Talk about the way the shepherd looks after sheep, finding fresh water and fresh grass, and protecting them from the dangers of wolves and bears. Sometimes a sheep will wander off on its own. (Send one of the sheep to go off and hide somewhere in the church, ensuring that enthusiastic sheep are prevented from going right outside.)

Jesus thought the way we wander off from living good lives was rather like sheep wandering off and getting lost. He loves all of us, and doesn't want any of us to be lost, so, like a good shepherd, he checks that all the rest of the people in the church are OK. (Are they?) Then he sets off to search for the one who has wandered off (see Luke 15:4-7).

As the shepherd searches for the lost sheep (tell him/her to wait with the sheep when it is found), give some examples of what makes us wander off from God. Perhaps other things crowd God out and take over our life; perhaps we want to disobey God's rules and please ourselves; perhaps some tragedy in our life shakes our faith, and we think God has caused the pain instead of realising that he is weeping with us. Whatever it is, once we realise we are a long way from God, we feel very lost and alone. Sometimes we have got ourselves trapped in habits we can't break out of on our own.

Thankfully Jesus, our good shepherd, is out looking for us, and he will search and search until he finds us. We can help by bleating – which is praying, calling out to God from where we are.

It is very good to be found. As the shepherd brings the wandering sheep, hand in hand, back to the flock, talk about how wonderful it is to know that we are forgiven, and that God loves us enough to forgive us even when we ran away from him. When the sheep comes back to the flock everyone can clap, as, with all the angels of heaven, we celebrate the truth that our God is such an excellent rescuer, full of understanding and mercy, and willing to give up his life to get us back home again.

Real goodness

Bring with you an egg cup, a whole egg in its shell, and a boiled egg which someone has eaten, so that just the shell is left, with a spoon hole at one end. Put this into the egg cup upside down so that it looks like a complete egg ready to eat. You will also need an egg spoon.

Begin by talking about those times you've desperately needed help, like missing the bus when you're already a bit late, or being caught in a downpour on your way to school, and you're hoping one of your friends will happen to drive past and see you. Perhaps the man who had been mugged in Jesus' story about the good Samaritan (see Luke 10:25-37) felt a bit like that, if he was still able to think after the beating-up he'd been given. Perhaps in the daze of his injuries he heard each set of footsteps coming nearer, and hoped that now he'd get some help. But no, the footsteps quickened up when they got nearer and then went off into the distance again. And the man still lay there, unable to move.

Perhaps he had almost given up hope when the Samaritan, a foreigner, stopped and came to peer at him to see what was wrong. Perhaps, as he swayed in and out of consciousness, he was half aware of being carefully given first aid, of being comforted and reassured that he was going to be all right. Those are good things to feel and hear, when you're in great need. You have no power at such times to make anyone care for you, so all you can do is rely on other people choosing to treat you well.

And that's what we're being taught today: that as Christians we are people called to treat others well, whether we're told to or not, whether anyone sees us or not, whether we want to or not. Why? Simply because our God says that this is the right and good way to live.

And the man in the Gospel, to whom Jesus told his 'good neighbour' story, could recite the rules he was supposed to live by off by heart: 'Love the Lord your God with all your heart and with all your soul and with all your strength and with all your mind. And love your neighbour as yourself.' But perhaps his life was a bit like this boiled egg. It looks wonderful and full of goodness. But if I start to dig into it (do that) with my spoon, I find that all the inside is missing, and there's nothing of any goodness there at all.

But don't be like a shell with nothing inside it. Make sure that the words your mouth says are backed up by the way you live. Come to God today and ask him to fill the shell with new meaning. He can do that, and he's waiting for you to ask.

Comfort or concern?

Arrange for the following items to be in church today, giving different people responsibility for them, so that they will emerge from various people all over the congregation: a pair of sunglasses, some well-known expensive brand of sun cream (the bottle can be empty), a luxurious, squashy cushion, a bottle of champagne (or a champagne bottle) in an ice bucket, and a CD player with some easy-listening music in it ready to play. At the front of the church you need one of those comfortable sun-loungers. Arrange for another person to walk quietly to the middle of the aisle with a begging bowl and sit down there.

Get the sun-lounger out and invite someone to be cosseted and pampered for a few minutes of the morning. They can lie on the lounger, and various people from all over the church bring them all their comforts. Enthuse about each item as you make the volunteer really comfortable. Leave them snoozing in luxury as you pose the question: 'Is there anything wrong with living in wealth and luxury, and pampering ourselves?'

In itself, no, there isn't. Of course it is good to have times of rest and relaxation, and it is fine to enjoy the good things of life. But if we use wealth to cushion ourselves from the real world, shield our eyes from the harsh glare of suffering, protect ourselves from feeling people's pain, block out the sound of people's crying, and deaden our sense of duty, then we run the danger of rejecting all the needs, and not feeling we have any responsibility to do anything about them anyway. (Hold a 'speech bubble' of card over the volunteer, which says, 'What problems?')

In Jesus' story about the rich man and Lazarus (see Luke 16:19f), the rich man was probably a nice guy, and there is no mention of him doing anything really evil. But he simply hadn't noticed the beggar who sat at his own front gate every day. Point out that all the time we've been enjoying indulging ourselves up here, there has been someone begging down there.

It's all too easy for us to ignore the needs. Jesus reminds us to check that our lack of poverty doesn't prevent us from doing the practical caring love we are called to.

True wealth

You will need the packing boxes for various consumables, such as a computer, electronic game, microwave, brand-name shoes, or luxury biscuits. You will also need such things as a CD, gardening and teenage magazines, and a film carton. Choose the items to suit the interests of the people in your congregation, and have enough for one person to hold all at once with great difficulty. Finally, you need a pocket Bible and a tiny spray of flowers.

Remind everyone of the story Jesus told in Luke 12:13-21, about the farmer who thought that having a bumper harvest, and therefore a financial windfall, meant total security, so that he could just do as he liked and take no care of his soul. His greed had made him foolish. As it happened, he was going to die and face God that very night, and he wasn't in the least prepared for death.

Ask for a volunteer to help you explain something. Explain how all the advertisements tell us that if we get a particular brand of yoghurt or car or shampoo, everyone will like us and fancy us, and we'll be really happy. Sometimes we get taken in by this lie, and start wanting to have things so we'll be safer or happier or better liked.

Go through the things we like to get, piling the packages into the arms of the volunteer as you talk. When they are completely loaded up, and have no hands left to hold anything else, point out the problem with all this 'having' being important to us. It means that when Jesus offers us his Word and his Love (offer the Bible and flowers), we simply haven't room to take it, and we turn it down, because our minds are too full of what we've got and what we want, and how we're going to hang on to what we've got.

And that is a tragedy that lasts not just for a few years but for ever. We need to put down our wanting and having, so that we can take the really important wealth that God offers us. (The volunteer is helped to unload, so they can hold the Bible and flowers.) These are the things which will make us content and happy and secure, whether we have all the other good things or not.

Mustard seeds

Have bowls of mustard seeds and invite people to take one as they come in. They can plant their mustard seed when they get home.

Ask everyone to look at the mustard seeds they were given when they came into church, and have a couple of tall people (or children on chairs) to stand back to back, spreading their arms out. In Israel, where Jesus was living, mustard seeds often grow as big as this, and local people will even use the mustard branches for firewood, so that tiny seed really does grow into a spreading tree, and all the birds love to sit in the shelter of its branches. The mustard plant provides spicy flavour, fuel and shelter.

Why did Jesus talk to the people about mustard? He often used things that were all around to help describe spiritual things which can't be seen. Perhaps there was a shady mustard plant right there where they were sitting, and some of its seeds scattered on the ground.

Anyway, Jesus said that the way God's kingdom grows is a bit like the way a mustard seed grows (see Mark 4:30-32). It starts off very little, and gradually grows very big. The little seed may be an act of kindness you do which makes someone think to themselves, 'I wonder! She's become a Christian, and it seems to be changing her for the better. Perhaps there's something in this Jesus person after all!' Or perhaps you're the one in the office who insists on honesty, even if you'd gain from being less than honest, and someone notices and starts thinking. Or perhaps someone notices that you aren't that impressed by the labels people are wearing, even though you're cool.

The little seed of God's kingdom is someone opening themselves up a tiny bit to the possibility of God being real and active in their lives. Gradually it grows in them. Perhaps they begin to ask more questions about God, perhaps they read some Bible stories or start coming with you to church sometimes. Then they start to pray! Now that little seed can really begin to grow, because God can lead the person step by step as they get in touch with him more and more. Sometimes the kingdom of God grows gradually as they pick up teaching week by week, or look at God's world with new eyes. At other times there's a sudden growth spurt. Perhaps a verse of Scripture hits home and they realise how their life needs to change, or they suddenly sense God real and close to them in a time of sadness or joy.

Perhaps over a few years, or a lifetime, that little seed has grown in the person until they are so full of God in their life that they are standing tall and strong in faith, and many come to them, now, for spiritual help and comfort, like the birds coming to the mustard plant's spreading branches.

How is the kingdom of God's growing coming on in us? Is it still a tiny seed, full of hope but not yet developed very much? Has it just started to sprout, putting out roots and shoots? Is it not growing very much at all at the moment, or has it recently had a big surge of growth and is excitedly stretching upwards and outwards in the knowledge of God's love and forgiveness? Or is it already tall and strong, providing spiritual shelter for others, scattering other seeds all around, and happy to be full of God's life?

What a world it would be, with churchfuls of people in it, in whom the kingdom of God was growing strong as mustard trees! It could happen. The people could be us.

Treasures old and new

Bring along something that is precious and old, and something that is precious and new. Choose items which your congregation are likely to relate to. (It could be a well-worn teddy and a new Teletubby for a baby, for instance, or an old stained-glass window in the church and someone's new engagement ring.)

First introduce everyone to the old thing, pointing out why it is so treasured and important and valuable. In our faith there are also ancient things which we as Christians value and treasure, such as the stories in the Old Testament which teach us about our God (for example, creation, Noah's flood, the great escape from Egypt, and the teaching of the prophets), and God's law, the ten commandments given through Moses to the people to help them live well and in line with God's will. Although these are old, ancient things, they are precious to us because they help us get to know God and live as his friends. We don't just throw them out because Jesus has come. Jesus valued them himself, and told his followers to go on valuing them.

Now introduce the new thing, explaining why it is treasured, important and valuable. In our faith there are also new things which we as Christians value and treasure. With the coming of Jesus, we are able to have a completely new kind of friendship with God that had never before been possible. Through Jesus dying, rising and returning to heaven, we are able to have the gift of God's life breathed into our own lives. That means that every new morning of our lives there are new possibilities in our daily friendship with the living God!

Not only are we looking forward to the coming of God's kingdom at the end of all time – we can also enjoy living in it now. In Matthew 13:31-33, 44-52 Jesus gave us some ideas of what the kingdom of God is like. Here is just one of them.

It's like some treasure you might find in a field. (You could have an exciting-looking treasure box there.) You're so excited about this precious treasure that you go and sell everything else you have, just so you can buy the field and own the treasure. Let's think about that. If you found a diamond ring, would you go and sell your house and car and World Cup coin collection to get hold of it? Probably not. You'd only bother to sell your house and car and cherished possessions if the treasure you had found was worth far, far more than all the things you already had. Jesus is saying that knowing God in a loving friendship and living in him each day is actually worth far, far more than anything else you own.

I don't think many of us realise that yet. It's as if we dig up a treasure box, look at it and think, 'Oh, that's interesting – a box of treasure. I'll pop over and look at it sometime.' Then we bury it again and go home to carry on living in the same old way without realising what we're missing out on. Next time you catch a glimpse of what God is really like, and how incredibly wonderful he really is, commit yourself to doing something about it, so you can enjoy that treasure of living in peace and love with him every day of the rest of your life.

Robes of righteousness

As people come into church make sure that everyone is given a small picture or cut-out paper shape of a robe of righteousness, with this title on it:

Probably we have sometimes looked into our wardrobes before a party and decided that we have nothing suitable to wear. However jam-packed the wardrobe is, with all that extra junk stuffed in to keep it out of sight, we can't find anything we want to wear! Prepare to be impressed: the wardrobe space of today's teaching is quite something.

Mention the piece of paper they were all given when they came in, checking for any who have been missed and providing for them now. Everyone has been given a beautiful wedding garment! That's what used to happen when guests were invited to palaces. It was the practice for kings to provide thousands of guests with a suitable robe each from their vast wardrobes in which thousands of garments were kept ready specially for such occasions. (Dress a volunteer up in a clean white robe – a surplice is fine.) They had special servants to be in charge of those huge wardrobes.

In Jesus' parable of the wedding feast (see Matthew 22:1-14) we can imagine all the poor and the dirty straggling along to the palace in their smelly rags, and the people in charge of the king's wardrobes fitting up everyone with a clean, beautiful robe to wear, before ushering them into the grand dining hall. No doubt they felt different dressed like this – perhaps they even walked taller and were more polite to each other than usual! Then the king comes in to inspect his guests. (Perhaps everyone sits up straighter, like you do when someone important walks into assembly.) He is glad to see the palace full of guests who have accepted his invitation, because the original guests had refused to come. Everything is light and warm and happy.

Suddenly the king finds a guest who has accepted his invitation but rudely refused to wear the proper clothes provided. He's still in the filthy rags he came in, and the king has him put outside in the darkness with those who had chosen to turn down his invitation.

What is Jesus teaching us in this parable? One thing is that God is very happy to invite all of us to the Church of Christ and feed us here with love and rejoicing. So we can be happy together in God's company and enjoy ourselves in our worship. The other thing is that if we say yes to God, we do need to let him reclothe us, and not expect to go on wearing the rags of bickering and fighting, lying and cheating, self-indulgence and lack of self-control which we came in. That's why we always start our worship by saying sorry to God, and hearing his forgiveness, letting him clothe us with robes of righteousness.

Cancelling debts

First ask anyone who has never done anything wrong, *ever,* to raise their hand. Make it quite clear that doing wrong doesn't stop when you grow up, and it's a problem that we all have to deal with. In which case there's going to be another problem we need to deal with. What about when people do things wrong which hurt and upset us? It's bound to happen, and today we are given some very useful teaching from our Lord Jesus to help us with it.

Suppose someone lets you down, cheats on you, loses their temper with you and says some cruel unkind things, lets you down again, steals from you, makes you look stupid, and breaks something you've let them borrow. (Count on your fingers seven typical offences.) Peter goes to Jesus and says, 'Is seven times about the limit for forgiving someone? It seems fairly generous to me. You might as well give up on them after that, don't you agree? Or am I being a bit over-generous – more forgiving than is good for me?'

Jesus says, 'Actually, seven times isn't nearly enough! You need to keep on forgiving until you've lost count and just do it anyway.' And then he tells one of his stories to explain what he means (see Matthew 18:21-35).

Give a volunteer a sign to hold which says 'IOU millions'. The story is about a servant who owes loads and loads of money. He has a wife and children, and he's borrowed so much and has been using his plastic money facility so much that he's stacked up a huge debt to his master, which he can't pay off. The master calls for him (use another volunteer and give him a mobile phone or a smart jacket) and demands the money. The servant kneels down and begs (he does this) to be given more time to pay. The master feels sorry for the servant and lets him off the whole debt! Just like that! (The master draws a thick black line through the IOU.) How do you think the servant feels? (Collect ideas.)

Now that is what God has done for each of us. Ask them to think of all the things they've done wrong, perhaps which no one else knows about except them and God. Think of all the meanness, selfishness, pride, hypocrisy and so on that we have been forgiven completely by God. It's just as if we owed God millions of pounds (hold up the IOU) and God has drawn that line through it, setting us free from the debt.

So here is this happy, free servant, who finds a fellow servant owes him a few pounds. (Give another volunteer a sign with 'IOU a few pounds' on it.) And the same thing happens. The servant goes on his knees and begs (he does this) to be allowed more time to pay. But what does the servant do? He grabs him by the neck and shakes him (not too realistically) and has him thrown into prison until he pays up. What Jesus wants us to ask ourselves is this: Is it fair or right for the servant to behave like this? What do we think?

Next time we are not wanting to forgive someone, let's remember how God has treated us, and pass on that loving forgiveness time and time and time again.

Using God's gift

Beforehand place three boxes of different colours around the church. In the red box put five one-pound coins (cardboard ones are fine!), in the blue box put two one-pound coins and leave the yellow box empty.

We know that one day the world as we know it will come to an end. We know that life as we know it will finish. All the prophets and Jesus teach us in the Bible that there is going to be a Day of the Lord, when we will see Jesus in all God's glory, and all that is evil will not survive. That includes people. How we live now in our lives will affect what happens to us that day. We do need to know that.

When will it happen? We don't know the time or date; in fact, what we do know is that it will happen suddenly, without us having loads of time to change. That's why we need to live every day as if it were our last.

But God doesn't want us so scared of the last day that we can't enjoy life here. Jesus came to set us free from that fear, and, if we are walking through life as Jesus' friends, there is nothing to be frightened of, because it's only the evil and bad and selfish that will be destroyed; everything that is good and loving and honest will be gathered up safely for ever.

Jesus told one of his stories with secrets – parables – about making the most of all the gifts God has given us (see Matthew 25:14-30), and we need three people to help us with it. (Make sure that the third servant chosen has been warned beforehand that she will be told off in the story, and is confident enough to cope with that.)

In Jesus' story, a man is going on a long journey and, before he goes, he gathers his servants together and entrusts his property to them to look after. (Give five coins to one servant and send her off to find the red box. Give two coins to another servant and send him off to find the blue box. Give one coin to the last servant, and send her off to find the yellow box.) The man went off on his travels, and after a long time came back home. He called the servants to him to settle accounts with them. (Call the volunteers together with the boxes.) Let's see how the first servant has got on. (She opens the box and counts out to the owner ten coins. Be very pleased. Everyone can clap.) What about the second servant? (He opens the box and counts out four coins. Praise and applause.) What about the third servant? Tell everyone how this servant told the owner she was too scared to do anything with her gift, so she just hid it as it was. (She gives it back.) The owner was not pleased at all because the servant had not made good use of the gift she had been given. (Tell the servant off, and thank all the actors for their help.)

We all have gifts God has enjoyed giving us. Some of us are good at being friendly and welcoming, some good at looking after animals, working out money, ironing, or thinking out solutions to difficult problems. Whatever our gift is, we need to enjoy using it and making the most of it for the good of everyone.

Check your oil

Beforehand prepare some sticks with red paper flames stuck on the end.

Begin by asking who has ever been a bridesmaid or a pageboy at a wedding. Were any of them late for the wedding? Jesus once told a parable about some bridesmaids (see Matthew 25:1-13). Some were ready when they were needed, but some weren't.

Show the 'torches' which were used at that time. Material was soaked in oil and tied on to the end of sticks. When you set light to them they would burn well, so the bride and bridegroom, coming from the bridegroom's house in the evening of the wedding, could have their way lit by the bridesmaids' torches. (Have a bride and groom and some bridesmaids to show this, holding their torch sticks.) At least, they could if the bridesmaids had their oil with them.

The problem in Jesus' story was that half the bridesmaids hadn't checked their oil supplies, so when the bridegroom needed their torchlight, they were rushing off to buy more oil, and ended up being shut out of the wedding feast.

What is the hidden message in this parable? What is Jesus wanting us to understand?

He wants us to be ready, and have our oil supplies topped up, so that whenever the bridegroom returns, even if he takes longer to arrive than we were expecting, we will be there waiting, shining brightly in the darkness. Then the bridegroom can lead us all into the celebrations and the feast.

Fill the oil lamp and light it. God's Spirit is like the oil we need to keep us burning brightly with God's love. If we stop keeping ourselves 'topped up' by forgetting to pray and read the Bible each day, our lives will stop shining, just as the girls' torches went out. Then, if Jesus suddenly returns, unexpectedly, either at the end of time or in a situation where our bright Christian love is badly needed, we won't be able to help.

So Jesus is telling us to keep praying, keep listening and keep loving. That way, we'll be all ready whenever he needs us.

Miracles

Straightened up

Bring along a couple of long scarves tied together.

Ask a volunteer to help you explain today's teaching, and get them to stand on the scarf. Wind the scarf round the back of their neck, and join the two ends so that the volunteer is forced to stand bent forward, looking down in a fixed position. Looking sideways is quite difficult, and looking up and into people's faces is almost impossible. Remind everyone of the crippled woman in Luke 13:10-17, whose back was set into this position so that she had lived the last eighteen years of her life looking down at her feet, unable to see the world properly, or have a face-to-face conversation.

What Jesus did was to release her from this locked position. When he saw her he felt so sorry for her and longed to set her free. And when he placed his healing hands on her back and told her she could now move again (untie the scarf), she found that she could stand upright, and see all around and look into people's faces again! That felt wonderful, and she praised God for all she was worth.

Now ask for another volunteer, and tie them up in the same way. Explain how people can be just as crippled and stuck in their thinking and living, even though their bodies look and work quite normally. Habits of grumbling about everything, wishing for things we can't have, or being so set in our ways that when God asks us to help someone we see it as impossible because it doesn't fit in with our plans – these things can mean that spiritually we are stuck and unable to look up and around. So can spending all our time thinking of one thing, whether that is a hobby, an addiction, an ambition, our health or fitness, or even a person. If we haven't looked up to God's face for ages, we might find we're stuck in the 'head down' position.

God is offering to release us from such crippling habits. He is the one who can put his healing hands on our lives (untie the scarves) and set us free again. It feels so good, and no one needs to stay trapped any longer.

The ten lepers

Ask for ten volunteers and dish out 'bandages' for them to wear on arms, legs and head. Explain that they are lepers and, because the disease is thought to be very catching, they can't stay with everyone else here but must go and sit somewhere else. Direct them to a place separate from the rest of the congregation. As they go, tell everyone how the lepers of Jesus' day had to leave their homes and live right away from the villages and towns, and look after themselves. How must they have felt? Lonely? Left out? Guilty? Unacceptable? Frightened?

We may not have the disease of leprosy, but there are lots of people in our world, in our country and in our town – perhaps even in our church – who feel lonely, left out, guilty, unacceptable and frightened, like the lepers. People cry themselves to sleep and wake up feeling sad about the day ahead. People who have lost contact with friends, or whose loved ones have died, try hard to be cheerful when they have a big ache of sadness inside them. Lots of people are hurting, and longing for their life to be different.

That's how these ten lepers felt that morning when they saw Jesus walking along the road on his way to a village (see Luke 17:11-19). They couldn't come too close to him, but they came as close as they could, and shouted to him, 'Jesus, Master, have pity on us!' (This can be written on a sign so the ten 'lepers' can shout it out.) People still cry out to God in their hearts like this. Does God hear?

He certainly does! Jesus shows us what God is like, and what Jesus did was to tell the lepers to go and show themselves to the priest. Whyever did he tell them that? Because if you were a leper and you were healed, you had to show yourself to a priest, so he could check you over and pronounce you fit and well.

Send your lepers off to the priest, who has ten cards saying, 'I declare this leper is now CLEAN. Signed: Revd. John Hayward.' Tell them that when they have their certificate of health they are free to join the other people in the congregation.

If any of the volunteers decides to come and say 'thank you' you can of course use this and praise it. However, since they haven't actually been healed of anything, they will probably all sit down in their places. Tell everyone how one leper (choose one) came back to Jesus to say 'thank you'. All the others had been keen to talk to Jesus when they needed something, but they forgot him once he had sorted them out.

Let's make sure that when God answers our prayers, we don't forget to say thank you – even if his answer is not the answer we expect.

Lazarus

You will need an inflatable ball or a balloon, and, if possible, a dummy used for teaching mouth-to-mouth resuscitation. Otherwise, bring along a large baby doll.

Begin by asking everyone to breathe in deeply, hold their breath while you count to twenty and then let their breath out. They will all have noticed how much we need that air. By the end of just twenty seconds we're getting desperate! Most of the time we breathe in and out without even thinking about it. Although it's such a vitally important thing to do, we're designed so that the breathing mostly goes on automatically so we can do lots of other things at the same time. Yet without that breathing we wouldn't be able to do any of those other things because we would be dead. That's how important breath is – it's a matter of life and death.

Ask a volunteer to demonstrate what we have to do if we come across someone whose breathing has stopped. Point out that what is happening when we are doing mouth-to-mouth resuscitation is that we actually do the breathing for the other person. With our living breath we can save someone's life.

In John 11:1-44 there is an amazing story of Jesus actually bringing someone back to life. It was his friend Lazarus, and when Jesus' voice, as the Lord of life, broke into the place of death, Lazarus heard his name being called and walked out into life again towards that voice.

Jesus calls each of us by name. He calls into the place we are, even if that place is full of darkness and sadness, or if the noise of unimportant things we like wasting our time on nearly drowns his voice, or if we're running as fast as we can away from God's way of living. Wherever we are, Jesus keeps calling because he wants to bring us out into new life. He knows his breath in us will transform our time in this life, and beyond that into the time after our physical death. As Jesus breathes his life into us it will make such a difference to us that we'll wish we'd gone for it ages ago!

Ask someone to blow up the ball or balloon, and as they do so point out what a difference it is making to have that breath inside. Once they are filled with our breath they have a whole new dimension – they're much more useful and they're much more their true selves. It's the same with us. When we let God breathe his life into us every minute of every day, we become much more our true selves, our life has a whole new dimension, and we are of more use to God in caring for the world he loves.

Jesus feeds the people

Begin by asking people how they like to spend their pocket money. Invite representatives of all ages to join in this. Has anyone ever spent their money on something which has let them down, or been disappointing, so that they end up wishing they had saved their money? Ask a few people to share their experiences.

It may be that you have had to watch as someone you are fond of wastes their money. You can see that it's all going to end in disappointment, or even tragedy, but they won't listen to you, and all you can do is stand by and wait to pick up the pieces when it all goes wrong, without saying, 'I told you so!' It's our love for the other person that makes us ache to see them wasting their money like that; because we love them we want better for them than to be sad and disappointed by things that aren't worth buying.

That's how it is with our parent God, who loves us to bits, and aches as he watches us spend not just our money but our time and our love on things which are not going to be good for us, or satisfying or rewarding. He wants better for us than that. God wants us to be aware of our need for his love and power in our lives, and to come to him for it, because he is happy to give it to us free.

Look at all those people in Matthew 14:13-21. Why had they bothered to leave their towns and villages and walk miles out into the country? They bothered because they knew their need of Jesus and were prepared to 'spend' their whole day looking for him and listening to him, hanging on his words. What did Jesus do? Did he let them down or disappoint them? No! He was there for them, ready to heal the sick friends and relations they had brought, ready to reassure them that God loved them, and teach them about how they could best please God in their lives.

And when their tummies started rumbling, and they knew physical hunger as well as spiritual hunger, what did Jesus do? He fed them! All he used was what they had. That's what he always uses. Are you a three- or four-year-old, ready for Jesus to use your life? Then that's what he'll use to make lots of other people really happy. Are you a seventy- or eighty-year-old, ready for Jesus to use your life? Then that's what he'll use to bring blessing and hope to lots of other people. And it's the same with all the rest of us in between.

What about our church? Is St Martin's ready to be used by Jesus? If we are, he will use us, and lots of people in this area will be blessed and given hope; if we aren't, and can't be bothered to go and spend time seeking Jesus out and listening to him, then he won't be using us and the people in our area will lose out.

Let's make sure that doesn't happen. Our job is to make ourselves available, and help give out to the people the gifts of God, so that all are properly fed.

Little things make a difference

If you have an ancient building you can direct people to look at how steps or pews are worn away by generations of people simply walking on the step or holding the end of the pew. Or you could show a well-used copy of a Bible, worn out and falling apart just by being handled and read every day. (It is said that Bibles which are falling apart are read by people who are not.) You could show an old and well-loved teddy, threadbare through daily loving.

Each step, each picking up of a book, each cuddling of a bear is in itself only a slight action which we can't imagine would do much. But day by day over the years, the effect of all those little actions starts to show quite dramatically. Little actions turn out to be very important. Even a smile can spread wider than we might think. There's an old children's poem about that:

Smile awhile, and when you smile
another smiles, and soon
there's miles and miles of smiles
and life's worthwhile
because you smile!

In John 6:5-9 we are told about one boy and his packed lunch. What was the point of him offering that when there were so many thousands of people to feed? Perhaps we think he might as well have just eaten it himself! But look at what happened when, instead of that, the boy wanted to offer what he had to share. Jesus used it. He blessed the gift that was offered and then all the people were fed, with some left over.

Those who have been God's friends for a long time will have noticed that God is very good at giving us more than we asked for, and giving in ways we hadn't thought of! But he does need us to offer what we have, whether that's time, money or talents and skills. Basically what we have to offer is ourselves. And when we do that, God can use the rest of our life here in ways we haven't even thought of, blessing people who perhaps we haven't even met yet, and may not meet till heaven. If we offer ourselves at the start of every day, the every day can be used for some wonderful good that wouldn't otherwise happen.

Walking on water

If you know a juggler, invite them to come and juggle as part of today's talk. Failing this, give out some balloons to a group of older children and ask them to keep them in the air, in as controlled a way as possible, using hands, head, knees and feet.

As the juggler or children perform, draw attention to the way they need to concentrate and keep their eyes on the balls or balloons if they are to be sure of catching them under control. Notice how the moment they lose concentration, or lose balance, things go wrong.

In Matthew 14:22-33 we hear about some people in a boat, weathering a terrible storm. It was the disciples, and Jesus had sent them off home while he himself went off to pray on his own after he had fed all those five thousand people. He needed to be alone with his heavenly Father to talk that over, and give special thanks for all that had happened. The waves were churning, and the boat was rocking and the disciples were frightened – especially when they saw Jesus walking across to them. This was water, and you can't walk on that! We are told they thought Jesus must be a ghost, and they got more scared than ever.

Let's look at what Peter did next. He called out to Jesus, 'If it really is you, then tell me to come to you over the water.' Why did he say that? What was he doing? It sounds as if he was testing whether Jesus was real or not, like us saying to a friend, 'If you've really been up in space, show me a photograph to prove it', or 'If you really love me, how about helping with this washing-up.'

Jesus knows he isn't a ghost, and he takes Peter up on what he's asked. 'Come on, then!' he says. There's no way out now! Peter concentrates on Jesus, like the juggler concentrated on the balls. He gets as far as climbing out of the boat, and he starts to walk towards Jesus, still concentrating on him, and then suddenly it all hits him. 'This is crazy! This is impossible! The water can't possibly be holding my weight! Rationally I know I ought to be sinking!' And as those doubts make him panic and lose his sight of Jesus, he does just that – he starts to sink and has to shout out in terror to Jesus to save him. And, of course, Jesus reaches out to him and gets him to safety straightaway.

Trusting Jesus is keeping ourselves concentrating on him and his love, underneath everything else that we do. Suppose you're buying some sweets. At the same time you're aware of Jesus and his love. What difference does that make? You will probably buy without being greedy, and you'll probably end up sharing what you get. Suppose you are travelling to work, and you've also got your eyes on Jesus. That will affect the way you drive, and the way you treat other commuters.

Today Jesus is saying to each of us, 'Yes, it is OK for you to put your total trust in me. Just keep that in mind and all the things which make you feel frightened and insecure will not let you sink – you can walk straight over them, confident in my love and power.'

That's life

The ingredients of life

You will need to spend a little time making a cardboard 'machine'. Beg a washing-machine/tumble-drier carton and cut out a machine outline using a craft knife. It might look something like this:

Set it up before the service, propped up against a table which has a washing-up bowl on it. You will need bags of flour and sugar, a tin of chocolate powder and a packet of chocolate biscuits, a couple of large potatoes, a bottle of cooking oil and a packet of crisps. You will also need an old twisted piece of metal (a scrunched-up metal clothes hanger will do fine) and a friendly, willing small accomplice to sit out of sight behind the machine.

Begin by explaining that you have brought along a machine which makes things. If you put in flour, sugar and chocolate powder (do so – just dumping the packets in, wrappers and all) the machine starts work with a low humming sound (which the children or everyone can do). And then the humming stops and out comes ... (the child behind hands you a packet of chocolate biscuits) . . . these!

If you feed in potatoes and cooking oil, the machine starts humming and then produces ... a packet of crisps. Explain that our lives are a bit like this machine; if we put into our lives lots of lies and arguments and thoughtless behaviour and gossip (drop in pieces of paper with these written on) then by the end of our lives we'll turn out like this ... all hard and bitter and twisted (the scrunched-up coat hanger).

But if we feed into our lives 'making an effort to be kind', 'forgiving people who hurt us', 'spending time with God' and 'reading the Bible' we shall naturally turn out a happy, free, loving person . . . (at this point the small accomplice climbs out and runs to give his/her parent a big hug). If we seek God and really believe that his love can make a difference to our lives, we're bound to become loving people quite naturally, and words and ideas will become increasingly in harmony with the God we worship.

Wearing masks

Introduce the talk with this short sketch:

Pauline Carter is sitting at her office desk working and answering the telephone. She can have the script in front of her, so she won't have to learn it.

(Phone rings. Pauline answers it in bored, automatic voice.)

Good morning, Pauline Carter speaking, how can I help you? . . . *(Suddenly sits up straight and adjusts hair, changes voice to be very efficient, and respectful.)* Oh Mr Townsend, good morning. How can I be of assistance? . . . Yes, certainly, I'm sure that would be convenient . . . I'll just check the date . . . Yes, Monday at 11.40 would be fine . . . Certainly, I'll arrange that . . . And you, too, Mr Townsend . . . Thank you so much . . . Goodbye.

(Carries on working. Phone rings again. Pauline answers it in efficient, friendly mode.)

Good morning! It's Pauline Carter here. How can I help you? . . . *(Suddenly raises eyebrows and slumps back in seat, getting on with work while the other person talks. She's obviously not really listening.)* Ah . . . oh, hi . . . mmm . . . ah . . . ah . . . no . . . look, I'm really busy here . . . yeah. OK . . . Bye. *(Carries on working. Phone rings again. Pauline answers it in bored auto voice.)* Good morning. Pauline Carter here. How can I help you?

Bring along a couple of different masks and ask volunteers to come and put them on. Point out how Farouk has now turned into a fierce tiger, and we might be scared of him; Mazin is now a clown and looks even funnier than usual! Thank the volunteers and restore them to their normal identities.

One of the things that all grown-ups do is to put on different masks for different people. We need to learn from the children, especially the very young children, how not to. What sort of masks do grown-ups wear? Not usually animal or clown masks, but masks all the same!

Like the woman answering the phone in the sketch, we put on a special voice for people we want to impress, we wear special clothes and try to give the other person the impression that we are efficient, cool, witty, deep or dependable. Why do we do that? Because we know that most people are influenced by outward appearances, and most people are fairly judgemental. If we can persuade them that we are worth respecting, then we reckon they will be more likely to listen to us and take notice of us.

Is that how we want it to be? Think instead of young children, who simply act as themselves, and haven't yet learnt the game of pretending who they are. You can see in the direct look in a young child's eyes that there is something there which grown-ups call innocence, because they are real; and we all regret losing that in all the clever pretending and wearing of masks.

As Christians, we are called to break that destructive cycle. We are *not* to judge from outward appearances, or just be friendly and respectful to wealthy, important-looking people. For us it's different because we know that every person we set eyes on is made and loved by God. And if we treat every person with the respect and love which they deserve as God-made human beings, they won't feel that they need to put on masks when they are with us. We will be joining Jesus in allowing people to be who they are, so that they are helped to wholeness and integrity.

Selective hearing

You will need a sieve – either a culinary or a gardening one. Also some appropriate thing to sieve – such as flour or earth.

First talk about the way we tend to hear if someone offers us a second chocolate biscuit, a raise in our pay, or a special discount, but not if we're being told to clean out the rabbit, work late, empty the washing machine or make a dental appointment. As the saying goes, 'There's none so deaf as those who won't hear'.

Explain that what our minds do is to sieve information which comes in through the ears and the eyes. Produce the sieve and start sieving so that everyone can see this process in action. The holes are a particular size so that everything is sorted automatically. Big lumps are not wanted, so they won't fit through the holes. Fine flour or earth can get through quite easily. The rest only gets through if we process it a bit first (breaking it down to a suitable size) and if it can't be broken down (like stones in the earth or a free sticker in the flour) then it doesn't get through the sieve at all.

In just the same way we are selective about what we hear, and mostly that is very useful to us. It stops us being turned into nervous wrecks by the daily news items, for instance.

But sometimes we try to keep out what God is trying to make us hear. Just because it may mean us changing something in our lives, we treat it as a threat, and shut it out, when really it is helping us to get rid of a way of thinking or behaving which is not healthy to us or others, physically, mentally or spiritually. What we need is to have 'God's Word'- shaped holes in our sieves, so that God's Word can always get through.

Ambitions

You will need to bring along a Christening gift of some kind (Peter Rabbit bowl, silver spoon or locket), a 5 or 10 metre swimming badge, an item of school uniform, several cups or trophies, a graduation certificate or gown, and a driving licence, a few brown envelopes and a clock.

Ask for a volunteer to help take everyone on a whistlestop tour of a lifetime. Work through a person's life (you can call them the name of the volunteer), presenting them with the trophies which mark each stage of the climb to power and greatness. As a baby they are presented with special presents. As they grow up they start doing clever things like swimming and riding bikes. They wear special clothes to show they're old enough and clever enough to be going to school and learning loads more things every morning. Perhaps they have a hobby – in sport or music – and they do so well that they keep winning cups and trophies for it. As they get older still, they're off to university, and a few years later, here they are at their graduation. It's congratulations time again. And then there are the driving lessons and the practice and the extra insurance, and suddenly it's the test, and a smart new driving licence. All they need now is the car to drive. But the work's going well and the money's coming in, so they can buy all the things they've always wanted, and here are the bills to prove it. And then, after a good many years of work, this highly respected person is old enough to retire. They have become a powerful and important pillar of society.

The volunteer is now loaded. Help unload them and thank them for their assistance.

We all have ambitions; we all hope our lives will turn out like our dreams. We want to be successful, liked, appreciated, fit and good-looking. And often we secretly want to be best. Jesus sees all of our dreams, even the secret ones. He knew what the disciples had been muttering about on their way as they walked along (Mark 9:33-35). They probably hoped he couldn't hear, because, like all of us, they had a strong suspicion that discussing who had most status was not really Jesus talk. Jesus really didn't care if the important people disapproved of him. He wasn't out to impress anybody, or work his way up, or gain status – he was just there to get on with the work of loving people to wholeness.

And that's what he wants for his followers as well. He wants us to have that freedom, so we can get on with what's really important, instead of wasting our time and energy empire-building in our particular area, impressing people, or collecting status symbols to wear or drive in. What do they matter when we compare them with God's values? Let's learn to be happy and content with nothing but being last, being unnoticed and the servant of all.

Responsibilities

Invite people to share what jobs they are responsible for, including household chores, professional responsibilities and so on. Have people of all ages contributing so that it is clear that we all have responsibilities of some sort, whatever our age. You could also draw attention to those responsible for particular jobs in church, making it an opportunity for everyone to thank the flower arrangers, servers and choir, cleaners and pastoral team.

Point out that right from the beginning, when Adam was naming the animals, God has made us human beings responsible for looking after this world and each other. That is the important job that God has given us to do. If we all did our bit and everyone acted responsibly to the planet and to one another, under God's guiding hand, we would find that our life together here would be greatly blessed. People would have enough to eat, and many disasters and much suffering would be avoided.

So why doesn't that happen, when it seems such good sense for us to live according to the Maker's instructions?

The trouble is that we all let our own wants and selfishness get in the way. If we, as rich nations, started acting more responsibly, then things we've become used to getting cheaply would be more expensive, and we might have to make do with less. Our greed stops us acting responsibly. So does our short-sightedness, when we want 'lots, now!' instead of considering those who haven't yet been born.

It's even the same in our friendships and marriages. If we are responsible in these, we will be caring for the other person and looking after their needs, sensitive to their feelings and wanting to help them. If one or other or both stop doing that, the relationship becomes hurtful and wearing instead of rewarding. The answer may not be to get out of the friendship or marriage, but change our way of behaving with each other, talking things over with each other and with God, learning to be responsible again. It is grown-up and sensible to know that life can't always be happy, and the person we love can't always agree with us. Giving one another space, understanding that we all have bad days, forgiving one another and working at our friendships – all this is part of being the responsible people God created us to be.

He doesn't expect us to do it without help. God is there with us in all the bad patches as well as the easy rides, and as a community we are to look after one another properly, making sure we're all OK and coming to the rescue whenever someone isn't.

Brownie wisdom

Begin with this short quiz:

1. What is H_2O?
2. How many legs does a spider have?
3. What animal pretended to be Red Riding Hood's grandma?
4. What is the current exchange rate for dollars?
5. What do you call a cake made with eggs, flour and sugar but no fat?
6. Who scored for Manchester United in their last match?
7. What are nine sevens?
8. What comes straight after a red light?
9. What is another name for Rose of Sharon?
10. How many balls in one over?

(Answers: 1. water; 2. 8; 3. wolf; 4. check in newspaper; 5. sponge; 6. check in newspaper; 7. 63; 8. red and amber; 9. St John's Worthypericum; 10. 6)

Are the people who knew the answers to our quiz necessarily the wisest people here? No. (Though of course they may be!) Real wisdom is different from knowing lots of facts. Remind everyone of the Brownie story about the wise owl. The children are sent to her because they want to find out who will be the little people who do secret good turns all around their house, and wise owl tells them to go to a pond in the woods and recite a poem. (Any Brownies, present and past, can join in the poem!)

Twist me and turn me and show me the elf;
I looked in the water and there saw . . . MYSELF!

The owl had been very wise because she had been able to help the children understand a deep kind of magic – whenever they did their good turns, they would be not just Imogen and Rebecca, but real Brownies! And they'd go on being Brownies whenever they did their good turns, long after they'd become Guides and grown up and had their own children who were learning the wisdom of the wise owl!

Wise people are good to go to when you want to talk things over, but you don't want to be told exactly what to do. Wise people are those who really listen to you – to how you are feeling inside as well as what you are saying. Wise people think carefully before they speak, and like learning from their mistakes.

We could say that WISDOM is all about
Walking In Simplicity Dreaming Of More
or we could say that to become WISE we need to
Wonder and ask questions
Imagine
Seek God
Expect to learn from him

Special days

Advent

Bring in a washing-up bowl with some water in it and a mop. Produce a mug or two which you were using earlier and explain how these are dirty and need washing up. You hope the mugs won't be too embarrassed by being shown dirty like this in full view of everyone. They are very particular mugs and prefer people to see them clean.

We are often a bit like that. We like people to see us when we're proud of what we are like and what we are doing. We don't like it much if someone catches us screaming at the dog, telling or living a lie, or being lazy or greedy. Usually we try to cover up the things we do which we aren't proud of. Perhaps we'll make out it's someone else's fault that we're late or grumpy; perhaps we'll think up good excuses for wrong behaviour. We get so good at this that often we believe our cover-up stories and stop noticing that instead of pretending we're clean-living Christians, what we actually need is a good, thorough wash.

The people who came to hear John the Baptist (see Mark 1:1-3) were just like us. There were things in their lives which were wrong and selfish, and they had become used to making excuses for themselves till they were quite content to live with their bad habits and carefully groomed images. But John got them thinking. And as they thought about their real selves and what they were really like, they suddenly started to realise that they were like dirty mugs which needed a good wash. If they were washed clean, they could be free from all the pretending and cover-ups, and just be themselves again.

John told them it was quite easy to do – they just needed to name all those big and little sins aloud to God without hiding them, and choose to turn their back on that way of living. He said he would dip them right under the water in the river as a sign that their lives were being washed clean.

(Ask for a volunteer to come and wash up the mugs.) For some of them it must have felt very humiliating to do that in public, especially if they had groomed their images so well that they had kept their sins well hidden. And it must have been such a relief for others, who had worried about their sin for years and years, to have it washed away at last.

When they were all washed clean, like our mugs, without any need to hide from God or each other any more, John told them something very important. This washing was just the beginning; soon someone was coming who would be able to plunge them deep into the depths of the Holy Spirit, so they would be completely surrounded and filled with the loving God. And the person who would make that possible was coming very soon.

During Advent we can get ourselves ready for Jesus' coming to us, just as they did. We can look at what we are really like; how we really behave with others; recognise the parts of us that are real enough but we hope others won't see. Anything we find which needs washing away we need to confess to God, tell him how sorry we are about it, and the way we have made excuses, and choose to turn our backs on that way of living. You can talk to God on your own or go to your priest or minister and pray with them, especially if you feel you need some help with changing. But however we do it, we all need to come to God regularly for thorough washing and he is the only one who can make us clean and free.

Christmas

Start by giving everyone one minute to find out from and share with someone else something that went really well, or was really funny or was a complete disaster this Christmas. One thing all humans have always loved doing is talking together! Toddlers, children, young people, middle-aged and old people all love a chat. Even babies talk, in their own way. What would we do without the telephone, especially if we can't get out like we used to. With e-mail we can chat to people all over the world, and with television, radio, magazines and newspapers people can chat to us about anything and everything. Ground control can direct astronauts in space, pilots can be talked down to a safe landing, and surgeons can talk their students through complicated heart operations. Politicians can shout their ideas to crowds of people, and friends can whisper their secrets. All of this is the magic of words.

Why do we talk about Jesus as the Word of God (see John 1:1-14)w?

Whenever we use words we express ourselves.

Jesus expresses God, not in a speech bubble but as a human being like us, so that we can understand God in a better way than ever. God has always expressed himself, of course, so the Word of God has been there as long as God has – for ever. God *said,* 'Let there be light!' God *said,* 'Let there be stars and plants and animals, fish and birds.' God *said,* 'Let there be people in our likeness to look after the earth.' So it was the Word of God which spoke those things into being through love.

Then, at Christmas, the Word of God actually took shape itself – human shape. And his name was Jesus, which means 'the one who saves us'.

Epiphany

Beforehand, arrange for a knitter to bring a completed garment to church, together with a ball of wool and needles. Also prepare a large paper cut-out of a similar garment, which is folded up so that the first bit that would be made is the only piece showing. Alternatively use the actual garment, folded up at that point.

Begin by showing everyone the wonderful garment that the knitter has made and asking how long it took to make and who it is for. What did it look like at first, when they started making it? The knitter can show the ball of wool and needles, and do a couple of stitches. Hold up the needles with these stitches and point out that it doesn't look much like a jumper / scarf yet! But the knitter went on working at it, knowing that one day it would be ready.

God knew that one day everything would be ready for Jesus to come into the world, but he, too, took a long time making things ready. He started by calling one person, Abraham. (Show the folded garment, but don't refer to it – it is there to be visual reinforcement of what you are saying.) Over the years God went on to prepare all Abraham's family. (More of the garment is revealed.) Until over more years that family became one nation. (Reveal some more of the garment.) But God's plan still wasn't finished. He went on to include not one nation but all the nations and everyone in them. (Shake the whole garment out and display it.) Today is called the Epiphany because the word 'epiphany' means 'showing' or 'revealing' or 'manifesting', and when those wise men arrived at Bethlehem with their presents, God was showing or revealing himself not just to Abraham or his family, not just to the whole nation of Israel, but to all the rest of us in the world as well.

Whatever country you come from, whatever you look like and whatever language you speak, God is saying to us today that he is there for you and no one is left out. You don't have to have the right ancestors to know God. You don't have to pass any exams to know God.

We sometimes get so interested in the presents the wise men were bringing to Jesus that we forget what brought them there in the first place. It was God who called these wise men from other nations to be there when Jesus was still a baby, so he could welcome them as well. They were there representing all the nations, so when God welcomed them he was welcoming each of us.

Lent

Bring with you a compass, and a chart showing that there are six weeks before Easter Day.

Explain that in six weeks' time it will be Good Friday and Easter Day, when we will all be celebrating Jesus rising to new life that lasts for ever, after being put to death on the cross. That's such a very special, important thing to celebrate that the Church decided we all need a few weeks to get ourselves ready for it. Time to think carefully about what it means to be a follower of Jesus. Time to sort our lives out a bit. Draw attention to the change of colour in church – purple is quite a serious, thoughtful colour, to match our serious, thoughtful mood in these next six weeks, which are called Lent.

Why six weeks? We are told that when Jesus had gone to the river Jordan and been baptised by John, he went straight off into the desert hills, to spend 40 days, getting ready to tell everyone the good news of God's kingdom. He didn't get ready by reading lots of books and doing lots of homework, or talking to lots of people. He got ready by living very simply, even going without food, and letting God lead him into the areas he needed to think about. He wanted to spend time finding out what God really wanted him to do with his life.

So, as the Church, we're going to do the same. Today is the day we all set off into the desert for six weeks. What do you think we'll need to take with us? Produce various items of combat gear, and mountain-walking clothing and equipment. Then kick it all away. We're not going to need any of this. All we need is one thing – a compass. What does a compass do? It helps you walk in the right direction. We need a special compass that always points us in God's direction.

Explain that you happen to have just the compass we need, and produce a cross – a wall-hanging one is about the right size so that people can see it easily. This is a special compass for us to take into the desert of Lent with us. Hold the cross flat. It points us always towards God's love, and at the same time it points back at ourselves. We can't pretend in this desert. We've got to be honest to God about who we are and how we are thinking and feeling. That's the only way the compass will point us in the right direction. Are we ready for the desert of Lent?

The first step on our journey is to agree to live more simply for a while, and go wherever God takes us. We can spend this week doing that, remembering to use our compass every day.

Mothering Sunday

Begin by interviewing a couple of mothers, one young and one older, using such questions as: What do you like best about being a mum? What do you find hardest? How has being a mum helped you grow as a person? What advice would you give to a young Christian couple about to become parents?

Talk about the way we all need to look after each other in the unselfish, loving way which we think of as mothering, and how that is the way our loving God treats us. He doesn't smother us or stop us exploring our world and trying everything out, but he encourages us and guides us so we know where to walk safely. If we fall over and hurt ourselves in life, he's there to comfort us and make us better, and if we go off and get ourselves lost in bad or stupid behaviour, he comes to search for us until he finds us, calling our name again and again until we hear him and shout out, asking to be rescued.

When we are little, our parents have to dress us, because we can't do our buttons up or tie our laces on our own. A good way to remember that we are all called to look after one another in a loving, caring way, is to think about it as dressing ourselves in clothes of kindness, forgiveness and patience, compassion, humility and gentleness. As you say this, dress a volunteer or a rag doll in various garments. Finally, to bind everything together, we need love (a belt is tied around the other clothes).

So tomorrow, and every morning when you get dressed, think of yourself also putting on the clothes of kindness, forgiveness and patience, compassion, humility and gentleness, and tie everything together with love (see Colossians 3:12-14). That way we'll be learning to look after one another the way our God looks after us.

Palm Sunday 1

Ask about football matches people have watched which have been really memorable and exciting. If you happen to have any players in the congregation, ask them to talk about a particularly memorable moment of triumph, and how it felt to have the spectators sharing the exhilaration.

When Jesus rode into Jerusalem all the crowds were on his side, cheering, waving and singing, pushing for the best view, and excited not just with Jesus as a hero but at what was a turning point for their side – their country. There would have been some there on that first Palm Sunday who saw it as a political statement, others as religious revival, others as a festive carnival of some kind.

So why did Jesus ride into Jerusalem on a donkey?

He was doing something the scriptures had said would happen to the promised Messiah. This meant he was giving a very strong hint to the people about who he was. He was saying that the Messiah had now come and was entering the holy city of Jerusalem as a king. But instead of all the rich clothes and grandeur of an earthly king, Jesus was riding on a very humble animal that was often piled high with people's luggage and shopping. It was a bit like using a bicycle rather than a Rolls Royce, stretched limo or BMW.

All the crowds that day cheered Jesus, but a few days later, once he didn't look like a winner any more, many of the same people had turned against him and were yelling for his blood.

What kind of supporters are we? Do we support our team only when it's doing really well, or do we hang in there even after a run of lost games? Do we stick with our friends even when they go through a bad patch? Do we keep trying even when a marriage gets shaky? And, perhaps most important of all, are we happy to sing God's praise in church on Sunday but ignore him or deny him by our behaviour and language and choices during the week?

These are Palm Sunday questions which we need to ask ourselves today.

Palm Sunday 2

Beforehand, make two large, clear signs, one saying, 'Hosanna! Blessed is he who comes in the name of the Lord!' and the other, 'Crucify him!'

First remind everyone of the way the crowds welcomed Jesus as he rode into Jerusalem on a donkey. They were all giving him the red carpet welcome, throwing down greenery and their coats for the donkey to walk on, and waving palm branches as flags, cheering and singing. One of the things they shouted was from one of their traditional songs, which we know as Psalms: 'Hosanna! Blessed is he who comes in the name of the Lord!' (Everyone can shout this as loudly as possible.) It meant they were welcoming Jesus as the new King David; they were really excited, expecting Jesus to become their king and throw out all the Romans so they would be free again. They thought they really wanted God's kingdom (see Mark 11:1-10).

Sometimes we are like the people in this crowd. We get all excited by Jesus, and promise to work with him, and feel ready to do anything to help the kingdom come. 'Let your kingdom come! Let your will be done!' we pray and we really mean it. We work hard at our praying, and do our best to be loving and honest in the way we live. We give God the worship we know he deserves, and we give of ourselves simply because we are filled with love for him.

In Mark 15:12-14 we are told what happened to Jesus on Good Friday. It makes us very sad to hear what happened to our friend, and we might find ourselves thinking that we wouldn't have left him alone like his friends did; we would have been there for him; we would at least have prayed with him and not fallen asleep in the garden.

But the crowd remind us of something rather nasty. They weren't singing 'Hosanna!' any more. They were shouting, 'Crucify him!' (All shout this.) And although we wish it wasn't true, we all know there are times when we do that as well. Those times when we know very well what is the right and loving thing to do or say, and we want Jesus out of the way so we can be as unkind and dishonest as we like. It's hard work having Jesus there when we don't want to be loving, or humble, or obedient. At those times we don't much like his kingdom. Every time that happens we are joining the crowd which shouted, 'Crucify him!'

Let's remember that, and pull ourselves together when it next happens so that, instead, we shout with our lives, 'Hosanna! Blessed is he who comes in the name of the Lord!'

Good Friday

Have the London underground map printed out on the weekly sheet, or have some larger versions available to show everyone.

Look at the plan and talk about the way it is simple sign language to help us make sense of a huge complicated network of rails and tunnels criss-crossing under the streets. The whole thing is so enormous to understand that we need this simple map.

But when we travel on the underground it only works because, as well as the simple map in our hand or on the station wall, the real massive tracks are laid in all those dark tunnels, and the electrical power is surging through all the thick cables, and the tilers have been busy fixing tiles on the station walls, and the computers are busy checking where each train is so that they don't bump into one another, and those moving stairs, the escalators, are well oiled and running smoothly. Although all this doesn't show up on our plan of coloured lines and blobs, we only have to look at it and we know that all the real stuff is right there.

In a way the cross shape is like one of those plans. Draw people's attention to the crosses they can see around them in church. It is only a simple shape, and we can all make it ourselves by placing one index finger across the other. (Do that now.) When people say 'fingers crossed' what do they do? (Ask some people to show this.) Today it usually means hoping we'll be lucky, but a long time ago it was people making the sign of the cross as they prayed about something they were worried about. (We could go back to using the sign that way!)

Now if the shape of the cross is like the underground train plan, what is all the real, deep stuff that the cross reminds us of? Ask everyone to find or make a cross and look at it, as you tell them about the deeper meaning: God loves the world so much that he was willing to give up everything, and come and live with us in person as Jesus. That love led him to a cross where he gave up his life for us, taking all the selfishness and sin on himself, and stretching out his arms in welcome and forgiveness, because he so longs for us to be free.

Easter 1

Bring along a few fresh eggs in a carton, and a chocolate egg.

Begin by reminding everyone that we are here for an exciting celebration. Draw attention to all the flowers, and the cleaning that has been going on, and any banners or other special Easter decorations and symbols. What is it we're celebrating? That Jesus had died on the cross and is now alive – alive for ever!

Introduce the chocolate egg. For some reason we've been seeing a lot of these at Easter. No doubt some people gave some away. No doubt some ate one before breakfast! What have they got to do with Jesus? Why do we all like to give one another eggs at Easter time?

One reason is that people were giving one another eggs around the time of Easter long before they had heard about Jesus. This is springtime, and eggs are all part of the spring, with its promise of new life.

New life! That's interesting – we've been hearing about the new life that Jesus gives us. When people came to our country and told us about Jesus, they thought the egg was a very good way of explaining the Gospel, so they kept it.

How does an egg help us to understand the Easter story? Show everyone the carton of ordinary eggs, and hold one up on its own. What is it? (An egg.) What comes out of a fertilised egg like this? (A chicken.) Yes, it's a new life – in this case a chicken. An egg is the way new creatures come into being. And Easter is about Jesus being alive in a new way and making it possible for all of us to be given new life.

What does the inside of an egg look like? (It's got yellow yolk and some thick runny stuff which is white when it's cooked.) What are some favourite ways of eating an egg? (Gather suggestions.) So what is inside the shell turns into something quite different. Jesus' life now, as from the first Easter Day, is different. For a start, he's never going to die again; his new life isn't a life that runs out. Even though Jesus has now been alive again for nearly two thousand years, he is outside time, so he hasn't got old. And he isn't tied to space like us, so he can come and go without having to catch a bus or open doors. He doesn't have to be seen to be real.

Now break one of the eggs. When we enjoy eating an egg the shell needs to be broken; otherwise we wouldn't be able to get at the white and the yolk. When a chick is ready to live in the big wide world it has to crack the eggshell before it can climb out. What does that tell us?

Sometimes we want to hang on to things just as they are. We don't always want to change, even if change in our lives is for the best.

Will we let our shells be broken ready for the new life Jesus wants us to have? God is calling us out of our shells into a whole new, different way of living. It is the loving way of living, trusting in God with our heart and soul and mind and strength, and loving one another. That may mean that some of our habits and fears may, like shells, have to be broken before we can live freely in the loving way. The good news of Easter is that Jesus has already broken through death and sin, so if we hold on to him, he can bring us through the shell breaking and out into the light and space of day – a daylight which lasts for ever.

Easter 2

Bring along a hot cross bun, a chocolate Easter egg, an ordinary hen's egg, and one of those fluffy Easter chickens.

Ask a volunteer to take the first object (the hot cross bun) around the church so everyone can see what it is. As they go, explain that these buns remind us that because God loves us so much he was prepared to live among us in person, and go on loving us even when he was arrested, tortured and killed on a cross. It's in Jesus' life, and in his experience on the cross, that we can 'taste and see that God is good'.

Now for the next object (another volunteer does the rounds) which is . . . a hen's egg. The egg looks as dead and as a smooth oval stone, but we know better. We know that if the egg is fertilised, and kept warm by the mother hen, that hard shell will start to crack, and into the world will climb . . (a volunteer takes the chick around) a fluffy yellow chick, full of life! So the egg reminds us that what looked dead and hopeless on Good Friday (when Jesus' dead body was taken down from the cross, and it seemed he had failed as the Saviour) was actually full of new life, because on the third day after that, Jesus broke out of death to be alive for ever!

And so our last object (a volunteer walks the chocolate Easter egg around) is what we all enjoy having on Easter Day – chocolate Easter eggs. They're always bright and colourful, fun and delicious, and that's because Easter Day is party time for Christians! Today we celebrate the fantastic truth that Jesus Christ is Lord – love has won the victory over evil and death for ever!

Ascension

Begin by staging a Mexican wave, which runs through the whole church or assembly. Point out how it only worked so well because all of us as individuals were working together as a unit of energy.

Remind everyone of the events leading up to today, giving them a whistle-stop tour of Jesus' life, death, Resurrection and post-Resurrection appearances. Explain how the disciples needed that time to get used to Jesus being alive and around, though not always visible or physically present.

Now they were ready for the next stage in the plan. Jesus leads them out of the city and he gives them his blessing, telling them to hang around Jerusalem without rushing off to do their own bit of mission work. (Enthusiasm is wonderful but it can sometimes make us race off to start before we've got everything we need.) The disciples have got to wait because God is going to send the Holy Spirit to empower them and equip them for the work they will be doing. It will make it possible for the news of God's love to spread out through the world like our Mexican wave.

When Jesus had finished giving the disciples their instructions and his encouragement, we are told that the disciples watched him being taken into heaven, until a cloud hid him from their sight. Those are the only practical details we have, so we don't know exactly how it happened. But we do know that the disciples were in no doubt about where Jesus had gone, and they were full of joy and excitement as they made their way back to the city to wait for the Holy Spirit, as Jesus had told them to.

A lot of years have gone by since Jesus ascended into heaven – nearly 2000 years. But that isn't much if you aren't stuck in time as we are, and God isn't stuck in time. He's prepared to wait to give us humans the chance to turn to him in our lives, and we don't know the date when Jesus will return. We do know that in God's good time he will come back, and everyone will see his glory together, both the living and those who have finished the earthly part of their life.

In the meantime, we have been given the Holy Spirit, so that God can be with us in person every moment of our life, helping us and guiding our choices, steering us safely through temptations, and teaching us more and more about our amazing God. All he waits for is to be invited.

Pentecost 1

Bring along an electrical appliance and, if necessary, an extension lead. Alternatively, have a torch or game powered by batteries, and keep the batteries separate at first.

Refresh everyone's memory of today's dynamic event, with the disciples praying and waiting on God, and the early morning experience of his power coming to them like a rushing wind, or flames, searching out each one of them and touching them with the touch of God (see Acts 2:1-4).

It quite overwhelmed them, and left them fired up with excitement at what God is capable of doing in people. They were bursting to tell everyone else about it, and wanted everyone to share this sense of God actually living in them. It was quite different from knowing about God; it was even different from walking about in the company of Jesus. This was like being flowed through with new life that set them living, talking and working in a new way.

Show the electrical appliance you have brought. Explain what this thing is capable of doing, but point out that at the moment it can't do any of those things. It has everything in place to work in that lively way, but something is missing at the moment – it isn't linked up to the power supply. Would it help if the appliance knew exactly how electricity works? Not really. However much is known about electrical circuits and the power grid, that won't bring this appliance to life. What it needs is this. (Plug the appliance into the power supply and switch on.)

Now the thing springs into life, and all kinds of potential are activated. That's what it's like having God's Spirit living in us and flowing through us. It makes that much difference! Just think what our world would be like if we were all full of the power of God's Spirit. Just think what a difference it would make in the world if all those in churches today all over the world asked God, seriously and openly, for a fresh outpouring of the Holy Spirit!

So often we are like well-finished appliances or games, knowing all about God's power, but not wanting to have the power switched on in us, just in case. Just in case what? Our God is the true, living God of love and compassion and mercy. Which means that any power he sends to touch us and affect us, will be only and entirely good for us. God is longing for his Church to be 'live' with the active power of his Spirit; we may be in good working order, but we also need to have the power, so that we actually 'work'!

Pentecost 2

Cut flame shapes from red and orange paper (shiny paper is especially good), and have these given out to everyone as they come into church.

Remind everyone of how the Holy Spirit came, with the noise of a gale-force wind (the noise of which they can try making), and looking like fire, which split up into flames resting on each of those in the room (see Acts 2:1-3). (Everyone holds up the flame they have been given, so there are flames all over the church.) That was how it seemed from the outside.

Inside each person, what was going on?

- (Display an exclamation mark.) The disciples were stunned by this display of the power of God. God meant business, and was clearly way outside their control. God was in charge.
- (Display a red rose or a red heart.) They suddenly knew, at first hand, what God's love really meant. They felt full of it, and it made them very happy and excited. They wanted to tell God all about it!
- (Display an empty speech bubble.) They wanted to tell other people all about it too. They wanted everyone to know God like this, because they knew how wonderful it was. And God's love in them made them want to share the good news, rather than keep it to themselves.

God is still pouring out his Holy Spirit on people, every day. Wherever anyone seriously wants to have the powerful love of God living in them, the Spirit will come and fill them.

Often we don't really want God that close. This may be because we are scared of God being really powerful; but we forget that with power which is full of love and goodness we don't need to be afraid. Mostly we just aren't bothered enough to take God seriously. The disciples were spending all day in God's company, waiting and hoping for the Holy Spirit to come. How much time do we focus our attention on God?

If we want something really badly, it fills our thinking all the time. Suppose we really want a computer, or to be a ballet dancer, or to drive a car. We'll be reading all the advertisements and the magazines, spending out on lessons and working hard at them, making sure we're in touch with the experts and so on.

So if each of us, and all of us as a church, are impressed by today's reading, and serious about wanting a fresh outpouring of the Holy Spirit, what can we do?

We can really want more of God in our lives. We can want that when we wake up, all through the day, and when we lay our heads down on the pillow at night. We can want it so much that we start listening to God and getting our lives ready to receive his gift. We can put God at the centre, instead of somewhere squeezed in at the edge. And God will come to us, filling us with his Holy Spirit, and transforming our lives.

Trinity Sunday 1

Beforehand, prepare a cake. Also get together two eggs, a bag of sugar, a bag of flour and some margarine, and a mixing bowl, cake tin and wooden spoon.

Set the cake tin down and tell everyone that today we are going to have a cake again, because it is Trinity Sunday. So we are going to have a Trinity cake. Ask various helpers to bring the eggs, sugar and flour and margarine and place them in the cake tin.

Proudly present the cake, inviting everyone to take a slice, and let the children point out to you that you haven't got a cake at all. You've just got the ingredients. But isn't a cake just ingredients, then? Let them help you understand that you'd have to mix them together and cook them before you had a cake.

Now let it suddenly dawn on you that it's a bit like that with the nature of God. God is the Father who created the world, Jesus Christ who saved us, and the Holy Spirit who gives life to the people of God. But they aren't separate from each other, any more than these separate ingredients are a cake. To be a cake all the ingredients need to be co-operating and working together. Then they become something which is not eggs, flour, sugar and margarine. Produce the real cake and point out that you wouldn't say, 'Have a slice of eggs, flour, margarine and sugar with your cup of tea.' You'd call it by its name: a cake.

In the same kind of way, when we talk about God we are talking about our Maker, and we're talking about the risen Jesus who has rescued us from sin and death, and we're talking about the Holy Spirit who brings us into new life. We know that the word 'God' means all three persons in a wonderful harmony, a community which is still One.

Give the Trinity cake to whoever is in charge of refreshments after the service, so it can be shared out then.

Trinity Sunday 2

Prepare a very large cutout triangle, as shown.

Also have three equal strips of card and three paper fasteners, or bring three equal strips of a large-scale construction toy, with the appropriate nuts and bolts – basically any three things which can construct a triangle.

Start by asking a volunteer to help by making a triangle from the separate strips. As they work, do a commentary on the progress, observing the sides move in all directions until that final join, at which point the triangle is a strong shape, with each two sides holding the other firm. It's such a strong shape that it is used in building – bridges, towers, pylons, roof rafters, for example.

Why on earth are we looking at triangles in church today? Explain that today we are exploring the nature of God. Will we be able to end up by bedtime knowing all about God, then? No! Human brains aren't big enough to cope with understanding our great God completely, any more than your hamster can understand completely what it is to be human.

But as your hamster gets to know you and become your friend, little by little he will understand more about you, as much as a hamster can.

So, back to the triangles. Perhaps they can help us understand a little bit more about the great and powerful God of love. (Show your triangle.) We've seen how strong one three-sided shape can be. Suppose for a minute we look at the threeness and oneness of God as a bit like this triangle.

We know that there is only one true God, and here we have one triangle. We know God our Father and Creator, Jesus our Saviour and the Holy Spirit. (Turn the triangle round as you refer to each side.)

Whichever aspect of God we focus on, we are always looking at God in all his truth and fullness.

And there's another thing. The Son always directs us to see the Father, and the Spirit; the Father always directs us to see the Son and the Spirit; and the Spirit always directs us to see the Father and the Son. (Turn the triangle round as you refer to each side.)

Of course, our God is far, far more than a mathematical shape – the God of love and glory is much more than a triangle! But the way a triangle works can help us understand a little more of how, for God, it's no problem to be one God, who is also Father, Son and Spirit. It's as natural for God to be like that as it is for us humans to be able to be in one place and think about being somewhere else, both at the same time.

All Saints

Give everyone a sweet which is wrapped in coloured cellophane (or just clear cellophane). This is a special present to everyone to celebrate All Saints' Day. Ask everyone to unwrap their sweet, eat it while they listen to the talk, and keep the wrapper carefully.

We are tasting the sweetness of our All Saints' gift. What makes a saint is someone who tastes the sweetness of God's amazing love and savours it, enjoying it and thanking God for it. Living like that is what transforms their lives, so that when people are with them they know they are in the presence of God. They can detect God's peace, God's love and God's joy.

Now invite everyone to straighten out their wrapper and look at it. When we look straight at it we notice all the sticky bits and fingerprints. When we look not at it but through it, we see beyond all those. That's how saints are with their view of life. They are here in the real, ordinary world, some of it bright and breezy and some of it heavy with sadness, and a bit messy. But they keep looking through all the experiences of this life, using them to help them understand more and more of the love of God which shines through it all.

We are all called to be saints, set apart as friends of Jesus, walking through this life in his company and dying in his company. What about after that? The Bible tells us about all the rejoicing that goes on in heaven for those who have gone faithfully through earthly life (see Wisdom 3:1-9; Isaiah 25:6-9 and Revelation 21:1-5). It's difficult to describe heaven in ordinary language because heaven is so wonderful that it breaks the vocabulary barrier, and no one can find quite wonderful enough words to give us the full picture.

But we do have some idea. Some of the joy of heaven spilt out into the sky above the shepherds' field near Bethlehem the night Jesus was born, and that was full of angels singing and praising with great delight. Whatever it looks like, we can be sure that there will be a glorious sense of welcoming love and homecoming waiting for anyone who has spent their earthly life close to Jesus, loving God and loving those sharing the earth with them.